THE HEART
OF
JESUS

Unveiling His Eternal Love for Humanity

SAMEH SAIED

LOGOS ECHOES

Contents

About LOGOS ECHOES Publications
About the Author

For God So Loved The World
That He Gave His One And Only Son,
That Whoever Believes In Him
Shall Not Perish But Have Eternal Life.

John 3:16

PREFACE

Divine Love Unveiled:
The Transformative Power of Christ's Ultimate Embrace

The love of Christ for humanity is a central theme in Christian faith, embodying a profound and transformative affection that transcends time, space, and human limitations. This divine love, revealed through the life, teachings, and sacrifice of Jesus Christ, represents the very essence of God's relationship with humankind

At the heart of Jesus's love is its unconditional nature. Unlike human love, which can be conditional and fleeting, Jesus's love is constant and unwavering. It does not depend on our actions or worthiness; instead, it is a pure and selfless love that embraces all people, regardless of their flaws or failures. This is powerfully illustrated in the Gospel narratives, where Jesus reaches out to the marginalized, the outcast, and the sinner, offering them forgiveness and acceptance.

One of the most poignant expressions of Jesus's love is His sacrifice on the cross. Through His suffering and death, Christ took upon Himself the consequences of human sin, offering redemption and eternal life to all who believe. This act of ultimate sacrifice demonstrates the depth of His love—a love that is willing to endure pain and suffering for the sake of others.

Moreover, Jesus's love is transformative. It is not a passive affection but an active force that changes lives. It calls individuals to a higher standard of love and compassion, encouraging them to extend the same grace and mercy to others that they have received. This transformative love empowers believers to overcome personal struggles, heal emotional wounds, and foster reconciliation and peace in their relationships.

In addition to His sacrificial love, Jesus 's love is also a source of comfort and assurance. In times of doubt and hardship, His love provides a steadfast anchor, offering hope and encouragement. The assurance of being loved by Jesus instills a deep sense of security and belonging, reinforcing the belief that one is never alone, no matter the challenges faced.

Ultimately, the love of Jesus invites a response. It calls for a reciprocal love, urging individuals to live out His teachings by loving others with the same compassion and selflessness.
By embodying Jesus's love, believers contribute to a world that reflects His divine mercy and grace.

In summary, the love of Christ for humanity is a powerful and enduring force that shapes Christian faith and practice. It is a love that is unconditional, transformative, and reassuring, offering both redemption and a call to live a life of love and compassion. Through His example and sacrifice, Christ demonstrates a love that continues to inspire and guide believers in their journey of faith.

Introduction

In a world where uncertainty and suffering often cast long shadows over our lives, the quest for a guiding light that offers solace and hope is both profound and urgent. This quest leads us to the heart of Christ, a source of unwavering love and transformative power. In *"The Heart of Jesus: Unveiling His Eternal Love for Humanity,"* we embark on an illuminating journey to explore the depths of divine affection that transcends human understanding.

In Part one : *Divine Love and Its Manifestations: From Creation to Redemption* ,Our exploration begins with a profound examination of *"Understanding Creation: Divine Power and Love,"* where we delve into the foundational aspects of divine creativity and its intrinsic connection to God's boundless love. We will uncover how the act of creation itself is a manifestation of God's eternal compassion and power.

As we continue, we address *"The Curse of Death and the Healing Power of Christ,"* revealing how Christ's sacrifice offers liberation from the curse of death and brings healing to the brokenness of humanity. This segment highlights the redemptive aspects of Christ's love and the promise of eternal life.

In *"The Gospel of Luke and the Doctrine of Divine Love in Chapter Fifteen,"* we analyze the rich teachings of Christ as presented in the Gospel of Luke, particularly focusing on the profound lessons of divine love encapsulated in Chapter Fifteen. This section provides key insights into the nature of God's love and mercy.

Next, we explore *"The Nature of Pride and the Fire of Divine Love,"* examining how pride can obstruct our relationship with God and how the transformative fire of divine love can purify and renew our hearts. This section underscores the dynamic interplay between human pride and divine grace.

The discussion then moves to *"The Transformation of Divine Love"* and *"The Transformative Power of Forgiveness and Divine Love,"* where we investigate how divine love transforms lives and the profound impact of forgiveness as an expression of this love. These sections highlight the practical implications of living under the influence of divine love and forgiveness.

"The Path to Mystical Union with Christ" offers a guide to experiencing a deeper spiritual connection with Christ, exploring the journey toward mystical union and its transformative effects on the believer's life. We also consider *"The Nature of Fear in Relation to Love,"* addressing how divine love can dispel fear and offer security and confidence in God's promises.

In *"Revelations of Divine Love"* and *"The Nature and Revelation of Divine Love,"* we delve into the ways in which divine love is revealed to us and its nature as described in scripture and personal experience. These sections aim to deepen our understanding of how God's love is revealed in various dimensions of life.

We also reflect on *"The Indwelling of the Holy Spirit and Divine Goodness,"* exploring how the presence of the Holy Spirit within us is a testament to God's goodness and love. Additionally, we contemplate *"The Fiery Love of the Trinity"* and *"Unconditional Divine Love and Redemption,"* highlighting the passionate and unchanging love of the Triune God and its role in our redemption.

Finally, we embrace "*The Eternal Knowledge and Love of God*," acknowledging the profound wisdom and enduring love that define God's relationship with humanity. This concluding section offers a comprehensive view of how eternal knowledge and divine love intersect in the grand narrative of redemption and salvation.

Wherever the indwelling of Christ in our hearts is the greatest gift a human being can receive. It transforms our lives from one state to another, from darkness to light, and from slavery to freedom. *The part Two: Christ in Us: The Depth of His Love and Presence in Our Hearts* , invites us to explore the depth of this spiritual transformation and how it impacts every aspect of our lives .When Christ dwells within us, our relationship with God deepens beyond measure. We move from being mere servants to being children of God and His friends. This part highlights this intimate relationship and how it is nourished by the indwelling of Christ in our hearts.

We commence with "*Why does Christ dwell in our hearts?*" This fundamental question forms the crux of our exploration. We shall deconstruct this profound concept, delving into how Jesus Christ is not merely a heavenly being but chooses to reside within the hearts of believers.

Following this "*Infinite Divine Love and Human Unity*" Here, we delve deep into the essence of divine love, understanding how this love is the driving force behind Christ's indwelling. We shall also discuss how this love binds us together as one body in Christ.

In "*Understanding the Divine Mystery of Adoption*" Divine adoption is a cornerstone of Christianity. We will explore how as God's adopted children, we partake in the divine nature. This adoption opens new doors to understanding our relationship with God.

Then turns to "*Participation in the Divine Nature*" This title addresses the practical aspect of divine adoption. How can we participate in God's holiness, power, and love? And what are the implications of this participation for our daily lives?

"*The Advent of the Living God*" examines that Jesus Christ is the incarnation of the living God. This section of the part will explain how Christ's coming to earth was a pivotal historical event, and how He continues to come to the hearts of believers.

In "*Our Need for Christ's Indwelling*" Here, we will explore the human aspects of this topic. Why do we need Christ to dwell within us? And what voids does His presence fill in our lives?   We then explore "*Christ Jesus: The Source of Our New Life*" Christ is the fountainhead of new life for believers. We will discuss how faith in Him leads to spiritual rebirth and a radical transformation of our lives.

"*The New Life We Receive from Our Lord Jesus Christ*" offers a reflection on the practical implications of new life. What does this life look like? And what fruits does it produce?

In "*The New Birth through the Sacrament of Baptism*" We will consider the sacrament of baptism as a means of receiving new life. How is baptism connected to Christ's indwelling? And what are the symbolic implications of this sacrament?

"*Understanding Truth and the New Covenant*" examines the idea that Biblical truth is the cornerstone of Christian faith. We will discuss how understanding truth leads to freedom, and how the New Covenant is linked to Christ's indwelling in our hearts.

Finally "*The Nature of Salvation and the Role of Love*" focusing on how the Salvation is a free gift from God. This section of the part will explain how love is the essence of salvation, and how Christ's indwelling enables us to love as Christ loved us.

In conclusion, this Part offers a comprehensive view of one of the greatest mysteries of the Christian faith: Christ's indwelling in the heart. By exploring these profound concepts, we will gain a deeper understanding of our relationship with God, and of the spiritual journey to which we are called.

"*The Heart of Jesus: Unveiling His Eternal Love for Humanity*" is not merely a theological treatise but an invitation to experience the heart of Jesus personally and profoundly. It is a call to understand, embrace, and live out the eternal love that has the power to transform, heal, and inspire. Join me as we journey through these pages to discover a love that transcends all barriers and offers hope to every human soul.

Part One
Divine Love and Its Manifestations:
From Creation to Redemption

Understanding Creation: Divine Power and Love

Consider the vast expanse of the world, encompassing not only the grandeur of the universe with its countless stars and galaxies but also the intricate details of our planet and the diverse ecosystems it supports. From the sweeping landscapes and majestic mountains to the intricate web of life within every biome, this immense and complex world invites us to reflect on the totality of creation.

The magnificence of nature, including the vast oceans, the delicate balance of ecosystems, and the diversity of living organisms, prompts us to consider whether all these facets were created by God to remind us of His infinite power, wisdom, and majesty. Each element of the natural world, from the grandest vistas to the smallest creatures, showcases the Creator's boundless creativity and sustaining presence. This reflection on the world's expanse and its intricate details highlights the divine purpose behind all aspects of creation, leading us to recognize and appreciate the comprehensive nature of God's grandeur.

Reflecting on God's power, which governs all visible and invisible aspects of creation, leads us to consider the connection between divine power and love. The common question arises: "*Why did God*

[9]

create the world?" The visible world answers this question by demonstrating the divine goodness that brought everything into existence from nothing. The diverse and abundant array of creation—such as the multitude of stars and the vast expanses of sand—reveals the Creator's goodness and compassion. Everything was created from the void to showcase God's goodness, power, and love, characterized by boundless generosity.

Creation is not static; it continues to exist and thrive because of the life and motion bestowed by the Creator. God did not merely create the world but also established it with order, boundaries, and goodness. As it is written, *"The Lord has established His throne in heaven, and His kingdom rules over all"* (Ps.103:19).

Christian doctrine teaches that the Father is the Creator of all things through His Son, Jesus Christ, the Word and Sustainer of all. This profound truth, which surpasses human understanding, reveals that the Father created both the visible and invisible realms for the sake of His only Son. The purpose was for the Son to reveal the divine fatherhood and guide all creation. As the Apostle states, *"All things were created through Him and for Him"* (Col. 1:16). Similarly, *"For by Him all things were created: things in heaven and on earth, visible and invisible"* (Col.1:16). Thus, everything was created through the Son and is given to Him, meaning that *"all things were created for Him."*

The Father prepared creation to be the realm where divine love is revealed through His Son and the Holy Spirit. This revelation began with the creation of man in God's image (Gen.1:26), granting him an existence that transcends all visible and invisible beings, not through human power but through divine grace. As it is written, *"So God created mankind in His own image, in the image of God He created them; male and female He created them"* (Gen.

1:27). When man was created in God's image, this image included elements of communion. The divine image represents rational and spiritual existence, allowing man to understand his own essence and rise towards the ultimate truth—the Word, the Son of the Father. The Son, eternally begotten of the Father, reveals the Father to creation and guides it towards Him so that it may dwell in the Trinity, enlightened by divine revelation given by the Son and instilled by the Holy Spirit.

These foundations of divine love include the creation of man in the image of God and the revelation of the Trinity's life, power, and love through the Son. Creation receives this revelation from the Son in both the visible and invisible realms—bodily and spiritual. The stability of creation lies in the divine love revealed by the Holy Spirit, as stated, *"The Spirit of the Lord will rest on Him—the Spirit of wisdom and of understanding, the Spirit of counsel and of might, the Spirit of the knowledge and fear of the Lord"* (Isa.11:2).

The divine image given to man expresses God's love by embodying resemblance, interaction, communion, and union with the beloved. God instilled love in man's heart to elevate him through communion to a higher state than mere individual existence. Individual existence alone does not provide true fulfilment or real existence. As it is written, *"We love because He first loved us"* (1 John.4:19).

Without being created in the image of God, man would be incapable of loving God. Love and the image are inseparable; the image is the essence itself, while love is the force that drives man to seek communion. This is not limited to the sensory and bodily level but extends to the spiritual realm. Failure to love others results in a void, prompting the soul to seek fulfilment through personal desires, which only exacerbates the emptiness. This void, not filled according to the divine image, leads to selfishness, hatred, envy, and other sins centred around the self. As it is stated, "*If anyone says, 'I love God,' yet hates his brother, he is a liar*" (1 John. 4:20).

Yet, God's love for humanity is evident in His granting of the divine image, enabling rational, free, and communal existence. Knowledge comes both from within the heart, where the Holy Spirit works to provide understanding and spiritual insight, and from external sources. The Holy Spirit, the source of wisdom and the speaker through the prophets, illuminates the heart, allowing the divine words to resonate with clarity and understanding without prior knowledge or reasoning. This enlightenment is a manifestation of the divine light that reveals truth and guides the soul towards a higher understanding. As it is written, "*Your word is a lamp to my feet and a light for my path*" (Ps.119:105).

The Curse of Death and the Healing Power of Christ

With the burden of sin comes the curse of death — an affliction chosen by humanity itself. This curse splits the inner life into warring forces, marking the onset of internal death and decay. It severs the life-giving forces within us and shifts our perception from understanding the truth to pursuing desire. People come to believe that violence signifies bravery, bloodshed signifies power, and insults signify strength. When lust and pleasure dominate the mind, the pursuit of truth becomes secondary to the pursuit of pleasure. As the heart burns with desire, memory fuels the imagination with past experiences, igniting wild desires in the will. In this state, humanity nears the pit of death — a place where self-indulgence masquerades as life itself. This false life is what the apostle Paul referred to as *"the generator of death"* (Rom. 7:24).

Amidst this violent whirlpool, where a person, consumed by the flames of desire, revolves around themselves, Jesus Christ has provided the sole remedy. Despite our weakness, He has established the principle of *"self-emptying"* (Phil. 2:6-7) through His incarnation. As the apostle puts it, *"Christ did not please Himself"* (Rom.15:3), since self-pleasing is the beginning of turning away from God and chasing after vanity and false illusions. It reflects a heart's desire for its own glory, excluding God.

The death of the life-giving Lord on the cross was meant to demonstrate to weak and weary humanity:

1. The power of self-sacrifice that vanquished the fear of death.

2. The immortality of the new life that placed death, Satan, and hell under our feet.

Thus, we pray to the Lord, *"Crush his head under our feet quickly"* (Prayer of Absolution), and we do not stop there; we ask, *"Scatter from us his wicked thoughts and mental images."*

Jesus Christ, the compassionate and wise healer, pitched His tent among us (John.1:14). In Him dwelled all the fullness of divinity in bodily form. *"Indwelling"* signifies union, and *"coming to dwell"* signifies revelation. Just as the Lord of the patriarchs once dwelled among His people, He now dwells among us as the head of the body, from whom all members draw life and strength. Jesus, the Physician of humanity, sends the divine power of self-emptying from His victorious divine nature to every member of the one body—the Body of Christ, the Church. As a healer, He enters the pit of sin with us to lift us up, enters the divided heart to restore it to peace, and enlightens the fearful with the beauty and light of eternal life and the splendour of heavenly grace.

When we pray the words of the Holy Spirit in every word spoken to the Lord Jesus according to the command of the first psalm, which describes the righteous as those who *"meditate day and night on the law of the Lord"* (Ps. 1:2), the secrets of divine love are revealed to us. Jesus, who loves humanity even those blinded by sin, is seen as the shepherd who never sacrifices even one sheep but goes after the lost one (Luke.15:4-6). He is the light shining in the darkness for all the lost because in Him was life, and the life was the light of men. The light shines in the darkness, and the darkness has not overcome it (John. 1:4-5). The darkness is enmity and hatred, and thus John the Apostle says, *"God is light, and in Him is no darkness at all"* (1 John.1:5).

When Jesus Himself says that the city set on a hill cannot be hidden and that a lamp placed on a high stand gives light to the whole house (Matt. 5:15), He is subtly pointing to His humility and love. He is the light that shines from a high place, having been *"lifted up"* on the cross to send us the radiant beam of His redeeming love, fulfilling the divine saying, *"And I, when I am lifted up, will draw all people to myself"* (John.12:32). He was *"lifted up"* to raise us with Him so that we might see His glory and believe in Him.

The Gospel frequently recounts that Jesus travelled through towns and villages healing the crowds, like sheep without a shepherd. He is the true Physician who searches for the sick. He is *"the true Physician of our souls and bodies."* He seeks the needy because, in His burning love for humanity, He does not rest, waiting for those who come to Him. Jesus overturned the rules of royal life; He became the King who seeks His flock, the serving King who bends down to search for the outcasts, the unclean, the lost, those under the dominion of Satan. He is the lover of mankind who seeks the needy.

When the Evangelist John says, "*Let us not love in word or talk but in deed and truth*" (1 John. 3:18), he reflects the teaching of Jesus Christ, who did not come to speak of love but to demonstrate it through His actions. Zacchaeus, the tax collector, saw the depth of Jesus' love for him and thus felt the Lord's love for him and sought his hospitality. Jesus did not speak of love to Zacchaeus but, in the silence shared between them, Zacchaeus realized the necessity of repentance. Love is revealed without words, and hospitality is stronger than words.

Similarly, the Good Thief, crucified beside the Lord, perceived the innocence and purity of the crucified one, followed Jesus in His suffering, spoke the truth, and testified to Jesus' innocence. Even amidst the suffering of the cross, Jesus did not forget the thief, saying, "*Today you will be with me in paradise*" (Luke 23:43). With divine insight, Jesus saw the seed of love in the thief's soul, despite the thief's own sins of theft and violence. The cross stripped the thief of his cravings and revealed the purity of the crucified one. It was divine providence that he died with the Saviour and that the Lord went before him to welcome him into paradise. In paradise, the thief saw what was previously beyond comprehension, seeing the one who is a flame of love and who promised him paradise.

The lover of mankind did not enter paradise alone but brought the thief with Him, for love seeks nothing for itself (1 Cor. 13:5). Jesus, the lover of mankind, entered Samaria because He saw a heart thirsty for love in the Samaritan woman. He sat by the well, waiting for that heart, that empty vessel filled with bodily impurities, believing it held the greatest reward. Jesus longed to give the woman the water that causes no thirst but satisfies completely. When one is satisfied, the yearning for further satisfaction becomes a desire for the fountain of eternal life (John 4:14). Thirst is the price of what we do not have; it is the vision of water and the quest for it. Satisfaction is the desire to taste and to seek to remain in grace and strive for more, not out of lust but out of the contentment of abandoning everything that hinders. This involves several spiritual forces working together:

1. The desire to cling to the Lord.
2. The free abandonment of everything that hinders this attachment.
3. The denial of everything that obstructs attachment.
4. Praise and remaining in fellowship.

This is not satisfaction but, rather, satisfaction begins with the vision of eternal life. It is not merely desire or feeling or emotions but is the spirit's leap with its rational powers toward something greater — Jesus Christ resting in the Father's embrace and the striving to remain in that embrace. Thus, the pursuit of spiritual gifts becomes as insignificant as speaking of dust, while the pursuit of remaining in the fire of love becomes the pure gold the soul desires with steadfast love.

The Samaritan woman began to remove her veils when she heard Jesus speak to her as a Jew, and another veil fell when she heard Jesus offer her *"the gift of God"* (John. 4:10). What remained was dispersed when she sought a means, for she had no *"bucket."* The water was not the water of Jacob's well; it was not the old experience nor the ideas and visions of those who lived before us. Drinking from the old history lives in the past and remains imprisoned by it, for time, customs, and ideas — even the new ones — do not bring us closer to God.

As the apostle and teacher Jesus Christ said, food does not bring us closer to God (1 Cor. 8:8). When He said that the Kingdom of God is not about eating or drinking but about righteousness, peace, and joy in the Holy Spirit (Rom. 14:17), He confirmed that intermediaries cannot bring us closer to God. These intermediaries include:

- Types of food.
- Ritual washings according to Mosaic Law.
- The system and times of prayers.
- Fasting periods.
- Types of clothing.

These practices do not make us *"pleasing"* to God, for God was pleased with us when He incarnated and loved the human nature offered to Him by the Holy Spirit, the Comforter, to *"implant"* divine love through the last Adam (1 Cor. 15:45) and present to the Father a complete human being *"full of stature"* (Eph. 4:13) as the good Father intended when He planned the creation of the world.

When the Lord came to Sychar and was weary from His journey, He sat by the well around the sixth hour (John. 4:6) — the hour when He was crucified, declaring His love for humanity. There, by the well, He offered the promise of eternal life to a woman with *"five husbands"* (John. 4:18) and the sixth was not her husband, revealing a lover. The limits of divine love are boundless. The Lord did not require repentance for the woman to receive His grace. As the Church teaches us, *"He was overcome by His compassion"* and then *"sent us His arm, surpassing all power to dismantle all barriers."*

Love *"is patient and kind,"* it *"bears all things,"* and does not retreat. Love does not seek faults or sins; it does not see sinners as unworthy but as loved as they should be. Love never fails, even in the face of obstinacy and pride of thought and heart. It does not seek judgment but reconciliation, does not seek to judge but to forgive.

The Gospel of Luke and the Doctrine of Divine Love in Chapter Fifteen

In Chapter Fifteen of the Gospel of Luke, we encounter the profound doctrine of divine love. The chapter exudes the sweetness of love, as the Evangelist recounts, *"All the tax collectors and sinners were drawing near to Him to hear Him"* (Luke. 15:1).

They saw in Jesus a compassion and acceptance that were absent in the Pharisees, who burdened people with strict, unbearable rules. The Lord Jesus, in contrast, poured out His love for everyone, embracing even the outcasts because, as the Evangelist says, He *"welcomed sinners and ate with them"* (Luke 15:2). His love was like a powerful flood, unstoppable and overwhelming.

In the parable, the shepherd leaves behind ninety-nine sheep to search for the one that is lost. Love, as depicted here, cannot bear to lose even a single stray sheep. The Lord's own words highlight this: *"When he finds it, he puts it on his shoulders, rejoicing"* (Luke.15:5). This demonstrates the strength of love as He joyfully carries the lost sheep back.

The Apostle Paul stated, *"Love does not rejoice in wrongdoing,"* setting a clear boundary for love—it does not condone sin. Yet, Jesus offers more than just setting boundaries; He demonstrates a positive, proactive love that rejoices in the return of the lost and bears their burdens. This love is so powerful that it carries the weight of sin and exhaustion from the sinner's shoulders. Thus, Jesus, the *"Lover of mankind,"* bears every sinner, regardless of their transgressions, embodying the essence of *"the Lamb of God who takes away the sin of the world"* (John 1:29).

The Lord Jesus emphasizes the joy of love in this parable. The shepherd, upon finding his lost sheep, calls his friends and neighbours to celebrate, saying, *"Rejoice with me, for I have found my sheep that was lost"* (Luke.15:6). He doesn't merely say *"the sheep,"* but *"my sheep,"* highlighting that the sheep's lost state does not diminish its belonging. This joy is not kept to oneself; rather, love, by nature, shares its joy, as it does not seek its own advantage. The Lord concludes: *"There will be more joy in heaven"* (Luke. 15:7).

The joy of love over the return of the lost is further illustrated in the parable of the lost coin, where the woman searches diligently for the coin she has lost (Luke.15:8). She lights a lamp to illuminate the darkness, symbolizing the enlightenment that love brings. After cleaning her house and finding the coin, she calls her friends to rejoice with her, showing that love not only seeks but also celebrates the return of the lost.

Love actively seeks out the lost and invites them back to God. It recognizes that a lost soul will remain lost unless actively pursued. This pursuit is twofold: searching for the lost, as shown in the parables of the sheep and the coin, and the act of love itself in seeking the lost person, as in the parable of the prodigal son, who *"came to himself"* and decided to return.

Love rejoices in restoring life, similar to how a farmer rejoices when gathering the harvest. Those who labour diligently *"reap with joy"* (Ps. 126:5), and the harvest comes with singing (Ps. 126:6).

When the seed of new life grows within us, the Lord fills our hearts and the hearts of the heavenly hosts with joy, as He has promised.

Love celebrates overcoming separation, as shown when the shepherd brings back the lost sheep and there is rejoicing in heaven. Love also triumphs over harshness, forgiveness over enmity, and peace over discord, transforming hostility into fellowship and mercy into reconciliation.

Love grants freedom of choice because where there is no freedom, there is no room for love. The father in the parable divided his inheritance and gave the younger son his share (Luke 15:12). Love allows freedom, even though the younger son squandered his inheritance and fell into poverty. Yet, the father welcomed him back with open arms, demonstrating that love does not hold grudges but rather embraces and forgives.

Evil knows no limits and is not bound by constraints. The younger son wasted his wealth, much like the first Adam squandered the image of God (Gen. 1:26). It is remarkable how dire need often arises in times of desperation (Luke 15:14). This reveals the inadequacy of human efforts to satisfy our deep spiritual hunger.

Humanity's search for fulfilment through paganism or adherence to the Torah often falls short. The Son of God came to remind us of the true richness available in the Father's house, bringing the message of the Kingdom. Despite the son's wasted inheritance and loss of dignity, the father welcomed him with compassion and joy, running to him and embracing him (Luke 15:20). This kiss symbolizes the profound love and acceptance the father extended to his son, despite his waywardness.

Love does not retain sins but casts them into the sea of forgiveness (Mic.7:19). The tenderness of love surpasses our failings, recognizing weakness without seeking excuses. Love does not judge but embraces and forgives.

The primary enemy of love is division, a fruit of pride and remnants of the old nature. Adam's desire to be like God, without sharing in the divine nature, led to his division and fall. He rejected being the image of God, becoming instead a reflection of himself, seeking self-existence and falling into death.

The Nature of Pride and the Fire of Divine Love

Pride divides because it involves the self's relentless pursuit of its own desires. This pursuit manifests as "*selfishness*," where the self seeks from within and through imagination what it believes is solely its own.

However, love is the fire that consumes pride, exemplified in the love of Jesus. Humanity often distorts and misuses the concept of love, applying it inappropriately or misunderstanding its true meaning. True love originates from the heart and is an internal vision and discernment, not merely a product of the mind. It is the foundation of living existence, transcending the temporary existence governed by mortality, which is characterized by desire and possession. In contrast, the existence renewed in Christ Jesus is marked by giving, transforming desire into a force for giving rather than a blindness to possession.

This concept reminds us of Psalm 23, a hymn of love. All psalms are songs of love, sometimes expressing sorrow from the troubles of enemies and sometimes seeking refuge in divine mercy to live according to that mercy. When we pray the psalms, we should pause, even briefly, to reflect on Jesus' love. Even in prayers for vengeance against enemies, these words mirror the old life inherited from Adam, which must be redeemed in the Last Adam, our Lord Jesus Christ, to whom be glory forever. Amen.

We have explored one aspect of love—emotions and feelings that sometimes surge like a powerful flood. These are branches of love but not its root or even its trunk. Sacred, noble emotions are good, but love is greater and more profound. It encompasses wisdom, insight, will, and vision, and is birthed from the warmth of the Holy Spirit and union with Jesus Christ. Sometimes this love is experienced through suffering and rejection, and other times in the glorious heights of Mount Transfiguration. This love comes from God's word, battles against evil forces, and endures through human trials. However, the path of the perfect is to generate feelings and emotions from wisdom rather than from mere sentiment.

When talking about the fire of the Holy Spirit, it felt like standing before a furnace of divine love. We observed that the flames moved harmoniously, purifying and instilling fear of sin, illuminating and strengthening our pursuit of truth, sanctifying us with a vision of the new life we yearn for, and delving into the depths of the human spirit.

This fire makes death seem less daunting than falling into sin, transforming love for enemies and forgiveness into sweet honey for the soul and body. At such times, we find no desire for sleep, speech, or socializing, but rather a profound joy in silence.

When the fire of the Holy Spirit touches our being, emotions and thoughts become insignificant; we no longer need them. As Job the righteous said, *"Naked I came from my mother's womb, and naked shall I return"* (Job. 1:21). The fiery love strips us of all that we know and seek, leaving us bare before the Holy Trinity. When the fiery spirit, strips us of self-preference over the Lord and others and unites us with the members of the Body of Christ, we enter the crucible of Golgotha. There, the self is ground into flour, which, transformed by the fire of the Holy Spirit, becomes the Bread of Life distributed by Christ Himself to the members of His Body. As the sacrificial Lamb and Bread of Life, He, through the Holy Spirit, unites us in His love, freeing us from passions and working with us to fulfil His heavenly will, as taught by the Apostle: "*Present your bodies as a living sacrifice, holy and acceptable to God*" (Rom.12:1).

The Transformation of Divine Love

The Lord transforms us out of His love, enabling us to become like Him. This transformation aligns us with the ultimate goal of love, which is our participation in the divine life of the Trinity through the glorified Son. As the Apostle John says, "*Beloved, we are God's children now; what we will be has not yet been revealed. We know that when he is revealed, we will be like him, for we will see him as he is*" (1 John. 3:2). This profound change allows us to share in the divine nature, reflecting God's love in our lives.

When we speak of the purification by the Holy Spirit, one of prayers asks: "*Give me the invisible fire to purify the weak.*" This divine fire reveals the eternal glory to us, strips away our attachment to earthly things, and helps the soul to appreciate and yearn for the new, beautiful life. Jesus promises in Luke 3:16, "*He will baptize you with the Holy Spirit and fire.*" This imagery underscores the transformative power of the Spirit, which cleanses our hearts and minds and enables us to embrace the new life with vigour.

Sanctification is not about removing what is alien to divine love but about our transformation into the essence of love, according to the extent of God's grace and our human capacity. This truth was revealed through the Incarnation of the Son of God, our Lord Jesus Christ. Paul writes in 1 Thessalonians 4:7, "*For God did not call us to impurity, but to holiness.*" This sanctification is a grace that renews us in the image of God as revealed in Jesus Christ, affirming our call to live in holiness.

The sanctity of the Holy Trinity is uniquely manifested through the Son by the Holy Spirit. It is this triune grace that restores us to the divine image renewed in Jesus Christ. Paul explains in 2 Corinthians 3:18, "*And we all, who with unveiled faces contemplate the Lord's glory, are being transformed into his image with ever-increasing glory, which comes from the Lord, who is the Spirit.*" The Father's call to "*Be holy*" is realized in the Son's act of sanctifying Himself for our sake (John.17:19), providing us with a unique experience of divine love that transcends ordinary perceptions and emotions.

The love of the Trinity is unparalleled, a divine love that surpasses all earthly bounds. This sanctified love is elevated above earthly concerns and requires us to seek this transformation through the fiery Spirit. As Paul states in Romans 5:5, "*God's love has been poured out into our hearts through the Holy Spirit, who has been given to us.*" This divine fire purifies our thoughts and alleviates the fear of judgment, guiding us to repentance not out of fear but from a profound experience of divine love, making our repentance pure like silver refined seven times (Ps. 12:6).

We see the signs of this sanctified love in our actions: those who cannot control their tongues or refrain from idle speech are distant from the love of God. Love heals rather than harms, as James 1:26 warns, "*Those who consider themselves religious and yet do not keep a tight rein on their tongues deceive themselves, and their religion is worthless.*" Injuries caused by words do not heal quickly but can deeply wound. Thus, those quick to condemn others have not truly encountered divine love. Paul advises in Ephesians 4:29, "*Do not let any unwholesome talk come out of your mouths, but only what is helpful for building others up according to their needs, that it may benefit those who listen.*"

Those who take pleasure in highlighting others' faults are far from knowing the love of God. Jesus teaches us in Matthew 18:21-22 that forgiveness should be abundant, saying, "*I tell you, not seven times, but seventy-seven times.*" Forgiveness is essential to divine love, and those who delight in others' failings are disconnected from this love.

When faced with condemnation, it's better to respond with love rather than just listening silently. Jesus instructs us in Matthew 7:1-2, "*Do not judge, or you too will be judged. For in the same way you judge others, you will be judged, and with the measure you use, it will be measured to you.*" By refraining from judgment and speaking in love, you align with the Father and the Lord who forgives and postpones judgment until the final day.

If fear of judgment overwhelms us, understand that it reflects remnants of the "*servant*" within us, which has not yet been renewed by Christ. Jesus, the Good Shepherd, offers comfort and healing, as promised in Matthew 11:28-29: "*Come to me, all you who are weary and burdened, and I will give you rest. Take my yoke upon you and learn from me, for I am gentle and humble in heart, and you will find rest for your souls.*" Place the remnants of this servant under the feet of the Lord, who became a servant for us (Phil. 2:7) to raise us to the glory of His Son-ship.

Do not think that God's love for us is measured by our understanding; this is a misunderstanding of divine grace. God's love is beyond our comprehension and exceeds the limits of our created nature. As Paul writes in Ephesians 3:18-19, "*May have power, together with all the Lord's holy people, to grasp how wide and long and high and deep is the love of Christ, and to know this love that surpasses knowledge—that you may be filled to the measure of all the fullness of God."*

The Incarnation of the Son, our Lord Jesus, demonstrates a divine humility that overcomes human pride and redefines our understanding of love. Philippians 2:7-8 explains, "*He made himself nothing by taking the very nature of a servant, being made in human likeness. And being found in appearance as a man, he humbled himself by becoming obedient to death—even death on a cross!*" Those who think God interacts with us based on our knowledge will face fear and judgment, as false knowledge binds love.

If we find ourselves trapped in faulty thinking about God, imagining Him as merely an exalted version of humans, we are engaging in a form of new paganism. Instead, we should return to the teachings of the Apostle, understanding the love of God that surpasses knowledge (Eph.3:19) through Jesus Christ. Jesus invites us to "*come and see*" (John 1:39), experiencing divine love rather than speculating intellectually.

Avoid asking "*How?*" as this question suggests a desire to follow an out-dated path of knowledge-seeking. Such love, born of mere knowledge, remains limited by human understanding. The true divine love, which the Holy Spirit imparts (Rom. 5:5), transcends intellectual pursuit and leads to a deeper, transformative experience of God's grace.

Thus, the fiery Spirit cleanses us of pride and fear, guiding us to a repentance grounded in divine love rather than fear. This repentance is pure and precious, reflecting the transformation wrought by God's love. Similarly, we should not dwell in fear but let it become a motivation to cherish and protect this love, avoiding self-centeredness and excessive self-love. As Jesus warns in Matthew 7:13-14, the narrow road leads to life, while the broad path leads to destruction. Those who focus on self will lose their life, while those who sacrifice self will find it, experiencing the divine love that teaches humility and reverence before God's boundless goodness.

The Transformative Power of Forgiveness and Divine Love

Jesus Christ, our Lord, died for sinners, and through His sacrificial death, He removed every corrupt love that leads to arrogance and self-centeredness. The cross has made a profound mark on history and our hearts, revealing that every person is a sinner. Without Christ, no one can truly experience genuine love—neither for oneself, for the world, nor for God.

Consider why Jesus emphasized that un-forgiveness prevents us from receiving forgiveness. It's not because God's love is conditional on our actions, but because un-forgiveness prevents us from experiencing the Father's forgiveness. As Jesus taught in Matthew 6:14-15, *"For if you forgive others their trespasses, your heavenly Father will also forgive you; but if you do not forgive others their trespasses, neither will your Father forgive your trespasses."* This is not a matter of divine harshness but of losing grace—the essential grace of forgiveness that helps us grow in understanding the Father's love. How can we bury this grace and expect to gain anything from it?

When we withhold forgiveness, our love remains restricted, unable to grow and even at risk of extinguishing under the weight of hostility. This barrier keeps us from fully experiencing the Father's love. Every action, thought, and feeling we engage with forms the foundation of our lives. Each one impacts us, either refining us with virtues or corrupting us with vices.

Thus, those with hardened hearts struggle to perceive or feel the transformative power of the Father's forgiveness.

From the story of the first Adam, we learn about the dangers of self-centeredness. Adam focused on himself and saw an independent self, disconnected from God, creating his own moral standards. This self-centred existence led to death and a severed relationship with the divine. Fear of death became a *"hidden disease,"* driving humanity towards false hopes of immortality. Consequently, human growth stalled because the self does not develop solely through its own abilities but through gifts received in divine communion. Love ceased, leading to violence and corruption, as exemplified by Cain's murder of his brother.

In contrast, the true Physician came, incarnated from the Virgin Mary and receiving His body from the Holy Spirit, to establish a new basis for divine communion, even in the physical realm. He emptied Himself to cover Adam's nakedness. As Jesus said in Luke 14:27, *"Whoever does not bear his own cross and come after me cannot be my disciple."* This call to self-denial is essential for entering the *"school of love"* and accepting the healing that restores our focus away from the self.

Denial of the self means rejecting the old life inherited from Adam to embrace the new life offered by the last Adam, Jesus Christ. Through His cross, Christ transformed humanity into a new, divine existence united with His Person. This union serves as a model and source for our own hidden union with Christ through the work of the Holy Spirit.

Denial of the self is a *"decision"* of the will, perfected by the anointing of the Holy Spirit. As 2 Corinthians 1:21-22 states, *"And it is God who establishes us with you in Christ, and has anointed us, and who has also put his seal on us and given us his Spirit in our hearts as a guarantee.*" This decision, guided by divine love, strengthens the human will to confidently embrace spiritual visions of new life.

It creates a longing for the glory of the Son of God, finding rest in His glory, despite conflicting emotions. The "*spiritual sense*" given by the Holy Spirit reflects the sense Christ's humanity experienced through union with the divine Word, and we receive from His fullness the grace that reveals the Trinity's love for humanity, as described in John 1:16, "*For from his fullness we have all received, grace upon grace.*"

Denial of the self is the foundation of true humility. When we acknowledge, "*We are sinners,*" we declare a fundamental truth. True humility is realizing our emptiness of goodness and recognizing that everything we have is a gift from divine enlightenment. As Romans 5:5 says, "*And hope does not put us to shame, because God's love has been poured out into our hearts through the Holy Spirit, who has been given to us.*" This humility leads us to be filled with the Holy Spirit, who pours love into our hearts according to His goodness and our frailty.

When the Apostle Paul describes love with negative attributes — such as not boasting, not being proud, not behaving rudely, and not seeking its own — he reveals the depth of the crucified love. For:

- The absence of envy comes from goodness.
- The absence of boasting stems from self-giving.
- The absence of arrogance signifies true humility.

- Not perceiving or proclaiming the ugliness of sinners reflects the love that led Christ, the Holy One, to die for us.
- Not seeking its own reveals complete forgiveness for all.

Consider the completeness of love:

- Love is patient and kind, and thus it does not envy.
- Love does not boast or act proud, and thus it does not seek its own.
- Love is not easily angered; it sees perfection before imperfection and remains a source of hope.
- Love does not think evil; it is pure and sees no evil.
- Love does not rejoice in iniquity; rejoicing in sin is the devil's joy, whereas the joy of love is the joy of God.
- Love rejoices in the truth, reflecting the Trinity: the Father rejoices in the true Son, the Son rejoices in the *"Spirit of Truth,"* and the Spirit rejoices in the truth declared by the Church.

Love bears all things because it has removed the barrier of sin that kept humanity from God. It believes all things, not out of naivety, but because love's purity cannot tolerate evil. All divine promises are true, and those who have experienced love trust in these promises. Love hopes for the perfection of everything and endures even for the prodigal son until he returns.

Thus, the Apostle Paul affirms, *"Love never fails"* (1 Cor. 13:8). Failure is confined to sinners, while falling signifies failing to achieve the ultimate goal.

The Path to Mystical Union with Christ

To achieve a mystical union with Christ, one must grasp and live by the law of love. This union begins with understanding the apostle's teachings on love as outlined in 1 Corinthians 13:4-8. Embracing this law necessitates a complete departure from sin, as sin inherently opposes love and, therefore, God. Sin obstructs every opportunity to experience genuine love by corrupting the soul, making it the centre and ultimate aim of existence. Consequently, it enslaves our senses to transient pleasures and narrows our thoughts to self-satisfaction.

Paul warns us about the destructive nature of sin, which includes envy, arrogance, suspicion, delight in others' misfortunes, and a quick temper — traits that mirror the devil's nature. The law of love, symbolized by the cross, is intended to bring about resurrection. The attributes of love described in 1 Corinthians 13 highlight that while love might be limited, the power of the cross overcomes these limitations. Jesus' act of forgiving those who crucified Him and His patience with Peter, who had denied Him, exemplify this transformative power. Rather than demanding an apology from Peter, Jesus simply asked, *"Do you love me more than these?"* (John 21:15).

The ultimate aim of the law of love is resurrection, which acts as a remedy for the *"hidden disease"* of self-centeredness. Resurrection imparts immortality through the Holy Spirit, redirecting our focus solely to the Father, through the Son, in the Holy Spirit. Paul, who understood the *"power of the resurrection"* (Phil 3:10), affirmed that *"love does not seek its own"* (1 Cor.13:5). When self-sacrifice becomes intrinsic, there is no longer a desire to seek personal gain. Instead, one's joy is found in worshiping the triune God, fully immersed in His love and unity.

In 1 Corinthians 13, Paul portrays the love of God the Father, revealed through Jesus Christ. This divine love transcends the old law given on Mount Sinai and written on stone tablets. It is now revealed in Jesus Christ, written on our hearts (Jer. 31:33), and empowered by the Holy Spirit, not by the mere letter of the law. Therefore, if we truly love Christ, we must teach others not to elevate any law above its ultimate purpose: the salvation of the lost and the repentance of sinners. The purpose of the law is Christ (Rom.10:4), who came not to condemn but to seek and save the lost (Luke. 19:10). And must cautious of those who, like the crowd that demanded Jesus' crucifixion, fail to recognize that the ultimate goal of the law is universal salvation. By not allow them to impose their harsh judgments on new believers, nor permit them to teach in a way that fosters a cruel and fearful image of God. True fear of God comes from the loss of fellowship, while misguided fear reflects a slave's dread of punishment, mistakenly believing that God is vengeful and waiting to pounce on every sin.

The Nature of Fear in Relation to Love

According to 1 John 4:18, "*There is no fear in love. But perfect love drives out fear.*" This profound statement reveals that where true love resides, fear cannot exist. Fear, which is often a remnant of our sinful nature, is like an old garment left behind at the threshold of divine grace. When the Holy Spirit plants the seed of love in our hearts, it grows and helps us to recognize the goodness of God, causing fear to retreat and be cast aside.

Fear brings torment and doubt because it undermines hope and obscures our perception of God's goodness. It is a lingering effect of sin, a "*deficiency*" rooted in the old human nature that trembled upon hearing God's voice in the garden of Eden (Gen.3:10). This fear resulted from a severed relationship with God, preventing true fellowship and intimacy.

The Scriptures speak of a sacred fear: "*The fear of the Lord is the beginning of wisdom*" (Prov. 9:10). While fear can be a starting point, it is essentially a sign of spiritual infancy. Many begin their spiritual journey with fear, driven by a dread of judgment, which can lead to repentance. However, this stage is not the final goal. Spiritual maturity involves progressing beyond this fear to experience the full measure of divine love revealed in Jesus Christ. Jesus teaches us that true wisdom is found not in fear, but in understanding and embodying divine love.

Those who are driven by fear of judgment are often not suited to guide others spiritually, as their love remains incomplete. Fear of judgment can harden hearts, leading to condemnation, rebuke, and even anger. This terror can morph into a desire to impose one's fears on others, mistakenly believing that such actions bring them closer to God.

When Jesus said, "*Do not judge,*" He illuminated the reason for our non-participation in judgment and exposed the corruption within our souls. He warned that "*with the measure you use, it will be measured to you*" (Matt. 7:2). This means that the standards we apply to judge others will ultimately reflect back on us, showing the importance of mercy and grace.

First, the measure of judgment we use often lacks true goodness and mercy. Second, it stems from a defensive posture and represents a "*wound*" inflicted by the "*hidden disease*" of death. Third, by applying this measure, we place God in our own judgment scale, which distances us from His fellowship and divine love. It is a grave error to lose the spiritual sense of God's goodness and mercy, which affects our inheritance in the spiritual realm.

Our actions return to us, bearing either goodness and righteousness or deficiencies and retreat from love. Love alone can restore the essence of the triune God within us, as it reflects the triune fellowship of mutual indwelling among the divine Persons. Each Person of the Trinity inhabits and resides within the others without separation or division, demonstrating that divine love transcends human division.

Since God's nature is love, distinctions between nature, essence, and Persons are intellectual tools for understanding. Each Person of the Trinity is unique, yet not separated but rather distinguished within the unity of divine essence. The Father is the source, and the Son is eternally begotten from the Father, revealing a love that transcends human comprehension. The Son, being equal in nature, is not lesser but fully equal, born from the same nature that is unified and singular.

The Holy Spirit is the gift of love from the Father to the Son, representing the Father's love for the Son. The Spirit proceeds from the Father and rests in the Son, as demonstrated in the Son's incarnation and baptism. This eternal indwelling of the Spirit in the Son created a place for His presence within us. When Jesus was anointed after emerging from the Jordan River, it was declared that He is the Christ, the Son of God (Matt. 3:17). As the Spirit overshadowed the incarnate Son on the mountain, the Father affirmed, *"This is my beloved Son. Listen to Him"* (Luke 9:35), confirming the heavenly teaching we have receive.

Love offers itself completely. Therefore, love involves the full giving of the Son's birth and the Spirit's procession. Both the Son and the Spirit give their essence entirely to the Father, just as the Father gives His essence fully to the Son and the Spirit. The wisdom of the Fathers used the term *"Person"* to articulate this complete giving. This concept harmonizes with the unity of divine nature, which is undivided and indivisible. The Trinity does not imply three separate persons added to nature but rather Persons within the divine nature itself, affirming that the Father is the source of both the Son and the Holy Spirit.

Revelations of Divine Love

What is revealed through this extraordinary and surpassing love?

The answer unfolds in three profound revelations:

The first revelation is the paternal love of God, which is all-encompassing and selfless. This love is depicted as boundlessly good, giving generously without any reservation. As we see in John 3:16, *"For God so loved the world that he gave his one and only Son, that whoever believes in him shall not perish but have eternal life."* This verse encapsulates the essence of divine love, which does not withhold anything but rather offers everything for the sake of humanity's salvation.

The second revelation is that the birth of the Son signifies equality within the divine love. There is no concept of inferiority or superiority in divine love. The love shared between the Father and the Son is equal, affirming the essence of salvation and eternal life. As stated in John 5:18, *"But Jesus answered them, 'My Father is working until now, and I am working.' This was why the Jews were seeking all the more to kill him, because not only was he breaking the Sabbath, but he was even calling God his own Father, making himself equal with God."* This passage highlights the equality of the Son with the Father, emphasizing that divine love does not recognize any form of diminishment or inferiority.

The third revelation is the procession of the Holy Spirit from the Father, which underscores the equality of the Holy Spirit with the Father and the Son. This processional act is a gift that the Father bestows upon the Son. As seen in John 15:26, *"But when the Helper comes, whom I will send to you from the Father, the Spirit of truth who proceeds from the Father, he will bear witness about me."*

This confirms that the Holy Spirit, who proceeds from the Father, is also equal to the Father and the Son. The eternal birth of the Son and the eternal procession of the Spirit reveal the Trinity in its unified essence.

The Father has revealed Himself as the Father of the only Son and the source of the Holy Spirit.

The Spirit is not born but proceeds, which signifies the distinction between the birth of the Son and the procession of the Spirit. The birth of the Son defines the destiny of humanity, providing adoption through the Son as a gift from the Father, in the Spirit (Gal. 4:4-6), *"But when the fullness of time had come, God sent forth his Son, born of woman, born under the law, to redeem those who were under the law, so that we might receive adoption as sons. And because you are sons, God has sent the Spirit of his Son into our hearts, crying, 'Abba! Father!'.*

This gift from the Trinity is a divine offering, emanating from the source, revealed through the Son, and given in the Spirit. The gift has three dimensions:

1. *It is a Reflection of the Son*: It mirrors the fellowship of adoption, modelled after the Son. As Ephesians 1:5 puts it, *"He predestined us for adoption to himself as sons through*

Jesus Christ, according to the purpose of his will."

2. *It is Spiritual*: It comes from the Spirit of life, the Spirit of the Father. Romans 8:16-17 states, *"The Spirit himself bears witness with our spirit that we are children of God, and if children, then heirs—heirs of God and fellow heirs with Christ, provided we suffer with him in order that we may also be glorified with him."*

3. *It is for All Members of the Body*: This gift is not exclusive to an individual but is extended to all members of the body, which is the Church. 1 Corinthians 12:13 says, *"For in one Spirit we were all baptized into one body—Jews or Greeks, slaves or free—and all were made to drink of one Spirit."*

The love of the Trinity operates within the divine life, akin to a circle, though not a closed circle. Unlike a circle, which is closed, the love of the Trinity is open to creation. It radiates from the Father, is revealed through the Son, and is given by the Holy Spirit. As in John 7:38-39, *"Whoever believes in me, as the Scripture has said, 'Out of his heart will flow rivers of living water.' Now this he said about the Spirit, whom those who believed in him were to receive; for as yet the Spirit had not been given, because Jesus was not yet glorified."*

The love of the Trinity floods forth like water from a spring, is revealed like water poured into a vessel, and is given freely. As 1 John 4:9-10 expresses, *"In this the love of God was made manifest among us, that God sent his only Son into the world, so that we might live through him. In this is love, not that we have loved God but that he loved us and sent his Son to be the propitiation for our sins."*

The love of the Trinity is inherently Trinitarian:

1. *It has a Source*: The Father is the source of this love.

2. *It is Revealed in the Son*: The love is made manifest in Jesus Christ, the Son of the Father.

3. *It is Given Through the Spirit*: The Spirit is the means through which this love is given.

It is crucial to understand that this love is a fellowship of love, not merely a love of an individual. As Jesus expressed in John 17:21, *"That they may all be one, just as you, Father, are in me, and I in you, that they also may be in us, so that the world may believe that you have sent me."* The divine love transcends mere individual affection and embodies a perfect fellowship that surpasses duality and excels in generosity.

The Father loves the Son and gives Himself to Him, and the Son reciprocates this love. This exchange is not limited to two but is open to a third person, the Holy Spirit. The Father's giving of Himself through the Spirit to the Son completes the circle of love. As 2 Corinthians 13:14 highlights, *"The grace of the Lord Jesus Christ and the love of God and the fellowship of the Holy Spirit be with you all."*

When considering the Trinitarian nature of love, it is illuminated through divine revelation as seen in the incarnation, baptism, and transfiguration of Christ. The incarnation from the Virgin Mary by the Holy Spirit, the baptism by John, and the anointing by the Holy Spirit reveal the Son as the beloved (Matt. 3:16-17) , *"And when Jesus was baptized, immediately he went up from the water, and behold, the heavens were opened to him, and he saw the Spirit of God descending like a dove and coming to rest on him; and behold, a voice from heaven said, 'This is my beloved Son, with whom I am well pleased.'".*

The transfiguration on Mount Tabor, where Jesus was overshadowed by the luminous cloud of the Holy Spirit, and the Father's declaration, *"This is my beloved Son; with him I am well pleased; listen to him"* (Matt. 17:5), further affirm the eternal son-ship and divine fellowship.

In summary, the divine love revealed in the Trinity is a profound, open, and communal love that transcends individual boundaries, offering a comprehensive and eternal fellowship to all who are in Christ.

The Nature and Revelation of Divine Love

Divine love is distinct and unparalleled, lacking any specific reason or cause, unlike human love which often seeks reasons and purposes. This divine love is characterized by its unity and continuous movement, manifesting through fellowship and generous giving.

We were created in the image and likeness of God (Gen. 1:26), which is why we naturally seek reasons and purposes. Before the fall, our purpose was to live in divine fellowship, embodying the love of the Trinity. This divine fellowship was clear and natural to humanity. However, after the fall, this clarity was lost. Knowledge became fragmented, goals became diverse, and understanding was separated from love. Consequently, knowledge conflicted with love until redemption restored both knowledge and the whole human being.

The redemption of knowledge is evident in both apparent and hidden ways. Apparent aspects include the purification of knowledge by love, which refines it from self-centred desires, aligning it with divine intentions. This is reflected in 1 Corinthians 13:8: *"Love never fails. But where there are prophecies, they will cease; where there are tongues, they will be stilled; where there is knowledge, it will pass away."* Knowledge finds its true purpose within love, which ensures it does not become barren or self-serving. Philippians 2:3 highlights this: *"Do nothing from rivalry or conceit, but in humility count others more significant than yourselves."* Additionally, the Holy Spirit renews love within us, giving birth to new knowledge that is illuminated by divine light, as stated in Ephesians 1:17-18: *"That the God of our Lord Jesus Christ, the Father of glory, may give you the Spirit of wisdom and of revelation in the knowledge of him, having the eyes of your hearts enlightened, that you may know what is the hope to which he has called you."*

The hidden aspects of the redemption of knowledge include the silence before divine mysteries, acknowledging that some things are beyond human comprehension as noted in Deuteronomy 29:29: *"The secret things belong to the Lord our God, but the things that are revealed belong to us and to our children forever, that we may do all the words of this law."* It also involves the abandonment of what is understood in pursuit of a higher, incomprehensible knowledge, aligning with 1 Corinthians 2:9: *"But, as it is written, 'What no eye has seen, nor ear heard, nor the heart of man imagined, what God has prepared for those who love him.'"* Astonishment and surrender before the divine lead to humility that makes all arguments and theories insignificant, as expressed in Job 42:3: *"Who is this that hides counsel without knowledge? Therefore I have uttered what I did not understand, things too wonderful for me, which I did not know."*

Divine love unites us with God, directs knowledge, and defines our union with Him. This fellowship is marked by both apparent and hidden signs. Those who have experienced God's love for sinners and understand His love in Jesus Christ recognize that this love is universal and individual. This reflection of divinity shows that love encompasses all believers uniquely, according to their growth and stature. John 3:16 confirms this: *"For God so loved the world that he gave his only Son, that whoever believes in him should not perish but have eternal life."* Love personalizes each individual, making them realize that their uniqueness prevents them from being anything other than a child of God. Romans 8:21 states: *"That the creation itself will be set free from its bondage to corruption and obtain the freedom of the glory of the children of God."* Understanding this freedom signifies deification and the rise above fallen nature.

The sanctification of the soul and body through the Holy Spirit makes each person a *"chosen vessel"* for love. This sanctification drives us towards ultimate submission to God, reflecting *"the likeness of Christ."* 1 Thessalonians 5:23 emphasizes this: *"Now may the God of peace himself sanctify you completely, and may your whole spirit and soul and body be kept blameless at the coming of our Lord Jesus Christ."* Experiencing the sweetness of eternal life while still in the body is a sign of fellowship with the divine. Colossians 3:2 encourages this perspective: *"Set your minds on things that are above, not on things that are on earth."*

The hidden signs of this divine fellowship are the joy in the Holy Spirit, the vision of the eternal Father, and harmony with the divine movement. Joy in the Holy Spirit signifies deep communion with divine love. Romans 14:17 highlights this: *"For the kingdom of God is not a matter of eating and drinking but of righteousness and peace and joy in the Holy Spirit."* Experiencing the glory of Jesus Christ and the manifestation of the soul and body by the Holy Spirit reflects the vision of the eternal Father.

Aligning with the movement of love within the Trinity represents a vision of the coming life that surpasses current understanding.

Joy in the Holy Spirit is the way of the crucified one who had crucified His will before His incarnation, becoming *"the pleasure of the Father"* and *"the Son of His love"* (Matt. 3:17). The Father is the joy of His divine Person, and the incarnate Son is also the joy of the Holy Spirit who prepared His human body and soul in the womb of the Virgin Mary. Thus, the joy of the Trinity is the joy of love in the incarnation of the Son, who *"gathered"* humanity into His divine, incarnate Person, making the human nature *"dwell"* within the Trinity forever. Jesus Christ, the Son of the Father, sought to establish this eternal life for us.

Joy in the Holy Spirit is the joy of the fellowship of the Holy Trinity's love. It is the joy of the Father in the Son, the Son in the Father, and the Father and Son in the Holy Spirit. The joy of the Holy Spirit in the Father and Son is the joy of each Person in the other. The first sign of this joy within us is the intense longing for prayer, solitude, and detachment even from sleep and food. This joy makes time pass unnoticed as it comes to us as a gift that the soul does not seek, avoiding the intrusion into the divine and falling into the illusion of having attained what is beyond our grasp.

The vision of the eternal Father is revealed to us through the illumination of the Holy Spirit. This divine vision is not a mere figment of imagination, nor is it solely the result of intellectual contemplation or an overflow of divine love in our hearts. Instead, it is the Holy Spirit's work that brings God's light into our minds, allowing us to perceive and appreciate the divine glory manifested through the love of the Father, the grace of the Son, and the fellowship of the Holy Spirit.

As we see in 1 Corinthians 2:10-12, *"These things God has revealed to us through the Spirit. For the Spirit searches everything, even the depths of God. For who knows a person's thoughts except the spirit of that person, which is in him? So also no one comprehends the thoughts of God except the Spirit of God. Now we have received not the spirit of the world, but the Spirit who is from God, that we might understand the things freely given us by God."* This passage highlights how the Holy Spirit imparts a deep understanding of divine truths, enabling us to grasp the profound realities of God's revelation.

The fundamental aspects of the Holy Trinity are central to our worship and understanding of God's revelation. In the Prayer service, we begin to experience these truths through the sanctifying grace imparted by the Holy Spirit. When we make the sign of the cross and hear the words, *"In the name of the Father, and of the Son, and of the Holy Spirit"* (Matt. 28:19), we enter into a sacred space where divine love and grace are fully realized.

John 14:16-17 further illuminates this grace as Jesus promises, *"And I will ask the Father, and he will give you another Helper, to be with you forever, even the Spirit of truth, whom the world cannot receive, because it neither sees him nor knows him. You know him, for he dwells with you and will be in you."* This promise underscores the Holy Spirit's vital role in guiding and sanctifying us.

The true essence of this divine call is realized through the Holy Spirit, who dwells within us, making the love of the Father and the grace of the

Son fully present in our lives. Romans 8:9 confirms this, saying, *"You, however, are not in the flesh but in the Spirit, if in fact the Spirit of God dwells in you."* The Holy Spirit's indwelling is essential to our sanctification and the fulfilment of our divine calling.

In summary, the vision of the eternal Father is brought to light by the Holy Spirit, who reveals the divine glory in the love of the Father, the grace of the Son, and the fellowship of the Holy Spirit. These profound truths form the foundation of our faith and worship, guiding us to a deeper understanding and experience of God's sanctifying grace.

The Indwelling of the Holy Spirit and Divine Goodness

The actions described by *"comes"* and *"dwells"* represent the work of the Holy Spirit. When we say the Spirit *"comes,"* it reveals its actions, and when it *"dwells,"* it bestows upon humanity the *"seal of eternal stability."* This divine anointing was first given to the humanity of the Lord Jesus Christ, inviting every person to receive this same anointing.

The Spirit dwells within us, imparting the spirit of love as stated in Romans 5:5: *"And hope does not put us to shame, because God's love has been poured out into our hearts through the Holy Spirit, who has been given to us."* The Holy Spirit lifts us from ignorance and softens the hardness of our hearts by revealing the humility and love of the Father.

As described in 1 John 4:9-10: *"This is how God showed his love among us: He sent his one and only Son into the world that we might live through him. This is love: not that we loved God, but that he loved us and sent his Son as an atoning sacrifice for our sins."* Experiencing this divine goodness and recognizing our true spiritual poverty makes the soul's contrition more precious than honey, as noted in Psalm 19:10: *"They are more precious than gold, than much pure gold; they are sweeter than honey, than honey from the honeycomb."* A soul that tastes God's goodness and His love for sinners can enter into a life of fellowship not through any personal righteousness, but only through the divine goodness that reveals the love of the Trinity.

Goodness is an eternal aspect of the Trinity's love. God is good and does not need anything from humanity nor demands anything in return. James 1:17 says: *"Every good and perfect gift is from above, coming down from the Father of the heavenly lights, who does not change like shifting shadows."* God's divine richness gives freely without asking, seeks the lost, and heals afflicted souls, as described in Luke 19:10: *"For the Son of Man came to seek and to save the lost."* Thus, for the sake of goodness, the Holy Spirit dwells in us, burning with a fiery longing for humanity, which has become united with the divine essence through the Incarnation of the Word, the only Son of the Father. 1 John 4:9 states: *"This is how God showed his love among us: He sent his one and only Son into the world that we might live through him."*

Goodness and mercy are inseparable. The goodness sought by the Samaritan woman is met with mercy that offers her salvation and the gift of *"living water,"* as mentioned in John 4:10: *"Jesus replied, 'If you knew the gift of God and who it is that asks you for a drink, you would have asked him and he would have given you living water.'"* These qualities are not merely attributes of the divine nature but are manifestations of that nature acting through love, which infuses creation with existence and life. Acts 17:28 says: *"For in him we live and move and have our being."* God embraces humanity at creation, unites it according to divine providence, deifies it by grace, and glorifies it in the Son through the Spirit dwelling in us.

The Spirit of the Father, who is also the Spirit of the Son proceeding from the Father (John.15:26), is given to us in Jesus Christ as the "*seal of adoption*" that remains forever. Ephesians 1:13-14 says: "*And you also were included in Christ when you heard the message of truth, the gospel of your salvation. When you believed, you were marked in him with a seal, the promised Holy Spirit, who is a deposit guaranteeing our inheritance until the redemption of those who are God's possession—to the praise of his glory.*" This Spirit is the prevailing love that sin cannot overcome. If rejected, it becomes a fire of judgment, as seen in Hebrews 10:27: "*But only a fearful expectation of judgment and of raging fire that will consume the enemies of God.*" However, if it dwells within us, it transforms into a fire of sanctification, as described in 1 Peter 1:2: "*Who have been chosen according to the foreknowledge of God the Father, through the sanctifying work of the Spirit, to be obedient to Jesus Christ and sprinkled with his blood.*"

The indwelling of divine humility enables us, despite our shortcomings, to cry out with Jesus: "*Abba, Father*" (Gal.4:6): "*Because you are his sons, God sent the Spirit of his Son into our hearts, the Spirit who calls out, 'Abba, Father.'*" We cry out through the Holy Spirit, who intercedes for us, presenting us as children of the heavenly Father because of humanity's redemption in Jesus Christ. This cry is a profound expression of paternal love that overflows with adoption, and through this cry, we are sanctified from all the defilements of servitude, as described in Romans 8:15: "*The Spirit you received does not make you slaves, so that you live in fear again; rather, the Spirit you received brought about your adoption to son-ship.*"

The Fiery Love of the Trinity

The extraordinary, fiery love revealed by the Trinity represents an unparalleled affection for humanity, surpassing all earthly understanding. This divine grace is a gift not extended to any of the heavenly orders, who are only faintly aware of their own fall and their unique relationship with God. Instead of taking on a heavenly nature to save the angels, the Word of God assumed human form from the virgin Mary , demonstrating an intense love for humanity. As the Evangelist John writes, "*The Word became flesh and made His dwelling among us*" (John. 1:14), affirming the Incarnation as a profound manifestation of divine love.

This divine love is characterized by its unbreakable unity. The union of divine and human natures in Christ is complete and unbreakable. This union was established to eradicate all forms of division and to forge an eternal and unending connection with humanity.

As Paul writes, "*In Christ God was reconciling the world to Himself*" (2 Cor.5:19), emphasizing that this unity is foundational to our relationship with God.

Furthermore, this love preserves the distinctiveness of each nature. While the divine nature did not relinquish its attributes, it elevated the human nature to share in divine glory. This is highlighted by Peter in his epistle: "*Through these he has given us his very great and precious promises, so that through them you may participate in the divine nature*" (2 Peter. 1:4). The Incarnation of the Son of God thus serves not only to glorify humanity but also to sanctify it, raising humanity to a new status.

The love of the Son of God does not involve any confusion or transformation of natures. Even though He took on the form of a servant, He, the Word, did not become a servant to the Father. Instead, He exalted the form of a servant to the status of adoption and glorified it. As Paul explains, "*He humbled himself by becoming obedient to death—even death on a cross!*" (Phil. 2:8).

Despite this real and eternal union, the divinity did not become humanity, nor did humanity become divinity. Such a transformation would undermine the mystery of salvation. The continued union of humanity with divinity is what grants humanity the new dignity of the Second Adam. Paul affirms this by saying, "*The first man was of the dust of the earth; the second man is of heaven*" (1 Cor. 15:47).

This fiery love for humanity establishes a profound and powerful prayer life, distinct from the experience of ancient peoples who felt abandoned by God. In the New Covenant, believers understand that any perceived absence of God is due to our own shortcomings, not to any deficiency in the Trinity. The Psalms reflect this understanding: "*How long, O Lord? Will you forget me forever? How long will you hide your face from me?*" (Ps. 13:1). This cry represents the experience of someone who saw the cross through prophetic vision but did not fully partake in the suffering, death, burial, and resurrection of the Lord in baptism. As the Psalmist wrote, "*My God, my God, why have you forsaken me?*" (Ps. 22:1), this cry is also echoed by Christ on the cross (Matt. 27:46), highlighting the depth of His suffering and the mystery of the divine plan.

When we recite these Psalms, we should remember that the foundation of our prayers lies in "*the mystery of the Incarnation of the Lord Jesus Christ,*" who came to us and was hidden in humanity, but not hidden from us. Jesus promises in John 14:18,

"*I will not leave you as orphans; I will come to you.*" He does not forsake us. However, the remnants of our old selves and our struggle to fully understand His love can make us feel abandoned. Yet, He has promised His perpetual presence and the indwelling of the Holy Spirit, the "*Comforter*" who stands as our advocate against the forces of darkness. As Jesus said, "*But the Advocate, the Holy Spirit, whom the Father will send in my name, will teach you all things and will remind you of everything I have said to you*" (John. 14:26). The Holy Spirit intercedes with the Father, bringing humanity into divine presence and ensuring that we are never alone.

Unconditional Divine Love and Redemption

Jesus chose to enter the home of Zacchaeus, a tax collector despised by his community. Zacchaeus was not liked because he collected taxes from his fellow townspeople, yet Jesus reached out to him. This act of kindness underscores a profound truth: God's love is not limited by human biases. Unlike our tendencies to favor those we like and shun those we do not, God's love embraces everyone equally. As John 3:16 affirms, "*For God so loved the world that he gave his one and only Son, that whoever believes in him shall not perish but have eternal life.*" This illustrates that God's love transcends human prejudices and extends to all people.

Peter once rebuked Jesus for speaking of His impending crucifixion, and Jesus responded firmly, saying, "*Get behind me, Satan! You do not have in mind the concerns of God, but merely human concerns*" (Mark. 8:33). Despite Peter's misguided words, Jesus did not abandon him. Instead, He warned Peter of his future denial but continued to support and restore him. In John 21:15-17, Jesus questions Peter three times about his love for Him, reaffirming Peter's place in the ministry despite his earlier shortcomings.

Even after receiving the Holy Spirit, Peter hesitated to minister to the Gentiles. Acts 10:9-16 describes a vision from God that was meant to overcome Peter's reluctance. Despite his reservations, God's love remained unwavering. Revelation 3:20 highlights this persistence: *"Here I am! I stand at the door and knock. If anyone hears my voice and opens the door, I will come in and eat with that person, and they with me."* This shows that God's love persists through our doubts and fears, always ready to welcome us.

Saul of Tarsus, a fierce persecutor of Christians, was transformed by God's love. Once driven by hatred, Saul became Paul, an ardent advocate of the Gospel. This transformation reflects the prophecy in Isaiah 42:3: *"A bruised reed he will not break, and a smouldering wick he will not snuff out."* God's love reignited Saul's heart, demonstrating that no one is beyond redemption.

Forgiveness is a crucial aspect of God's love, as taught in the Lord's Prayer in Matthew 6:12: *"And forgive us our debts, as we also have forgiven our debtors."* However, the greatest expression of divine love is our union with the Trinity. This is highlighted in 2 Corinthians 13:14: *"The grace of the Lord Jesus Christ and the love of God and the fellowship of the Holy Spirit be with you all."* This union represents the ultimate form of love and grace, far surpassing any worldly gift.

The fiery love of God is also evident in His miracles and in His care for the marginalized. Those who are often rejected by society are highly valued by God. In Luke 4:18, Jesus declares, *"The Spirit of the Lord is on me, because he has anointed me to proclaim good news to the poor. He has sent me to proclaim freedom for the prisoners and recovery of sight for the blind, to set the oppressed free."* This shows that God's love is especially present for those who are outcast or suffering.

Our prayers, even when they are filled with struggle, should be offered with love. Romans 5:5 assures us: *"And hope does not put us to shame, because God's love has been poured out into our hearts through the Holy Spirit, who has been given to us."* The challenges we face in prayer teach us that while our efforts may ebb and flow, God's love remains constant and generous. James 1:17 reminds us, *"Every good and perfect gift is from above, coming down from the Father of the heavenly lights, who does not change like shifting shadows."*

Reflecting on the depth of divine love, we see that the union of divine and human nature in Jesus Christ represents the highest calling. This union is not just about receiving blessings but about partaking in the eternal inheritance that God offers. Romans 8:16-17 declares, *"The Spirit himself testifies with our spirit that we are God's children. Now if we are children, then we are heirs—heirs of God and co-heirs with Christ."* This incredible gift of eternal life begins with baptism, marking our adoption into God's family — an unparalleled gift that transcends all earthly measures.

The Eternal Knowledge and Love of God

In the Scriptures, Jesus makes it clear that eternal life is defined by the knowledge of God the Father and Jesus Christ. This understanding goes beyond mere intellectual knowledge; it is deeply rooted in divine love, which invites us to become *"children of God,"* as stated in 1 John 3:1: *"See what great love the Father has lavished on us, that we should be called children of God!"* This intimate knowledge cannot be separated from eternal life and adoption. Jesus affirms this in John 17:3, saying, *"Now this is eternal life: that they know you, the only true God, and Jesus Christ, whom you have sent."*

The essence of eternal life is to experience love that transforms us from servants into beloved children. This is clearly expressed in Romans 8:15: *"The Spirit you received does not make you slaves, so that you live in fear again; rather, the Spirit you received brought about your adoption to son-ship."* There is no divide between knowledge, eternal life, and adoption; they are one in the divine love that makes us God's children. 1 John 4:16 reinforces this by stating: *"So we have come to know and to believe the love that God has for us. God is love. Whoever lives in love lives in God, and God in them."*

Understanding eternal love, knowledge, and son-ship means recognizing them as the manifestations of the Holy Trinity's distinct roles and the essence of divinity. The Son of God, beloved by the Father, reveals the Father to us and grants us eternal life. John 3:16 expresses this profound truth: *"For God so loved the world that he gave his one and only Son, that whoever believes in him shall not perish but have eternal life."*

This inseparable connection to holiness is also underscored in Hebrews 12:14: *"Make every effort to live in peace with everyone and to be holy; without holiness no one will see the Lord."* Holiness is not just a virtue; it is our participation in God's own holiness, enabling us to be *"blameless before Him"* as described in Ephesians 1:4: *"For he chose us in him before the creation of the world to be holy and blameless in his sight."*

Though our discussion has been extensive, it is crucial to understand that love involves more than the Father loving the Son and entrusting Him with everything necessary for our salvation. Through the

Son's appearance, we grasp the gift of adoption. As the Son expresses His love for the Father in John 17:6: *"I have revealed you to those whom you gave me out of the world,"* He also shows that He is our Redeemer, aware of our weaknesses but not ashamed to call us His brothers. Hebrews 2:11 declares: *"Both the one who makes people holy and those who are made holy are of the same family. So Jesus is not ashamed to call them brothers and sisters."* Just as a doctor comes to heal human wounds, Jesus is not ashamed of our sins.

We should confess to Him our lack of fervent love and our failure to ignite the fiery love the Spirit gives. 2 Timothy 1:6 reminds us: *"For this reason I remind you to fan into flame the gift of God, which is in you through the laying on of my hands."* We must seek that this fire of love motivates us day and night to cherish Christ above all, enduring hardships with the patience of saints, as Revelation 14:12 puts it: *"This calls for patient endurance on the part of the people of God who keep his commands and remain faithful to Jesus."* The patience of love is boundless and persistent, driving us to abandon everything to see the fulfilment of divine promises in Jesus Christ.

As we come forward, we should embrace the Lord with the same love He has shown us—a love that extends to the death of the cross. Philippians 2:8 affirms: *"And being found in appearance as a man, he humbled himself by becoming obedient to death—even death on a cross!"*. Because choosing to stay steadfast in love means prioritizing commitment over temptation and maintaining unwavering devotion.

Therefore, the church stands as a place where soul and body unite with Jesus Christ. Each service within the church should be our great celebration of union with the Lord, holding fast to love and surrendering all for this purpose. 1 Corinthians 11:26 states: *"For*

whenever you eat this bread and drink this cup, you proclaim the Lord's death until he comes."
This is what highlights the significance of the cross — the life-giving cross. This cross is the seal of Jesus Christ's love, confirming the eternal covenant with His blood. As Hebrews 13:20 notes: *"Now may the God of peace, who through the blood of the eternal covenant brought back from the dead our Lord Jesus, that great Shepherd of the sheep."* The resurrection signifies the power of the cross, demonstrating Jesus' victory over death through love. Marking oneself with the sign of love is a profound gesture. As the cross is completed with the invocation of *"and the Holy Spirit,"* it symbolizes a return to the eternal covenant, affirmed by the love of Jesus Christ through the power of the Holy Spirit. This practice underscores the connection between divine love and the sacred bond it represents.

In conclusion, growth in divine love is intertwined with the development of grace, As 2 Peter 3:18 instructs: *"But grow in the grace and knowledge of our Lord and Saviour Jesus Christ."* Growth in love stems from growth in grace, and growth in grace comes from our union with the Holy Spirit. He alone opens for us a new life in full, eternal fellowship and love.

Why Does Christ Dwell in Our Hearts?

Why does Christ dwell in our hearts? This is a question rooted in deep love, and it is the right question to ask. How He dwells comes second to understanding why He does. The Apostle Paul says, *"so that Christ may dwell in your hearts through faith,"* but he first stated, *"that He would grant you, according to the riches of His glory, to be strengthened with might through His Spirit in the inner man"* (Eph. 3:16). By using the word *"so that,"* Paul indicates that the gift of the Holy Spirit is the reason Christ can dwell in our hearts. Before asking how this happens, we must first understand why it happens. However, it's important not to confuse the concepts of *dwelling* and *indwelling,* as both terms are used in the Scriptures. *Indwelling* can be seen as a precursor to *dwelling.* The Apostle speaks of our Lord Jesus Christ: *"For in Him dwells all the fullness of the Godhead bodily"* (Col.2:9). Regarding dwelling, Jesus Himself said, *"We will come to him and make Our home with him"* (John.14:23), or *"abide with him."* This implies that the divine gift is not bound by words but defined by love. Therefore, Paul's statement about being *"strengthened with might through His Spirit in the inner man"* underscores that we cannot endure the full presence of divinity within us. Our human nature lacks the spiritual and physical strength needed to host God or the Holy Spirit. Instead, we receive three essential gifts from the Lord Jesus that allow Him to dwell in us, and us in Him.

The first gift is the gift of knowledge. This knowledge comes when our hearts are enlightened, allowing us to perceive the works of God. It is granted to us through the sacrament of holy baptism, providing us with divine light to strengthen our minds and comprehend the precious salvation given to us by the Lord.

The second gift is the gift of communion in the Lord's body, meaning we are considered members of His body, the Church. This gift is bestowed upon us through the sacraments of baptism and the Eucharist. Hence, the Apostle says, *"For by one Spirit we were all baptized into one body"* (1 Cor. 12:13). The Apostle affirms that being incorporated into the body of the Lord Jesus, the Church, qualifies us to receive the indwelling of the Lord by the Holy Spirit, along with all believers.

The third and greatest gift, for which the first and second gifts are given, is the gift of son-ship. The Apostle explains this by saying, *"Because you are sons, God has sent forth the Spirit of His Son into your hearts, crying out, 'Abba, Father!'"* (Gal.4:6). Through the mediation of our Lord Jesus Christ, the head of the new creation, and because He has united His humanity with His son-ship, thereby recreating humanity in Himself, as the Apostle states: *"If anyone is in Christ, he is a new creation"* (2 Cor. 5:17).

The new creation represents the human nature redeemed by the Lord, a new nature formed in the person of the Holy Spirit, the Son, and by the will and goodness of the Father. Therefore, this new nature is qualified to have the Holy Spirit dwell within it without being destroyed or suffering irreparable harm, because the Lord Jesus came not to bring death but to give life — an eternal life free from death and corruption.

Since the gift of son-ship is the foundation of all gifts from God the Father, we must affirm that this son-ship is that of the Son, our Lord Jesus Christ, *"the firstborn among many brethren"* (Rom.8:29). This son-ship, which we share, does not multiply or increase regardless of the number of believers. It is singular because the old nature and the first creation multiply through physical birth and increase according to the Creator's power. In contrast, the new nature multiplies through union and increases according to God's high and exceptional calling in Jesus Christ. Union is not measured by numbers, size, space, or time — these are metrics of the first creation. We may say a city has a population of ten thousand and count them. But in the mystery of Christ, we do not count by numbers; instead, we speak of *"one body."* The life of the one body is not measured by number but by union. This union is valued by the grace described by the Apostle as *"rich"* and by the purpose, which is to be in fellowship with the Holy Trinity and with the Holy Trinity for the glory of God the Father.

We are God's children by grace because the Lord Jesus brought this grace from the Father, through the unity of the undivided divine essence, which is inherently against division. He is one with the Father in essence but distinct from the Father as the eternal Son. This distinction does not involve counting or comparing, as numbers do not express the essence of God. Even when we say *"God is one,"* we do not refer to the number one but to *"unity."* Thus, the distinction of the Son from the Father is the basis for the distinction of believers, each distinct from the other according to the teachings of the Apostle, which describe the distinction of members of the one body according to the mystery of Christ (1 Cor. 12:11-12).

As we are distinct as members of the one body, we are also distinct from the Son, which is a distinction of grace. We are not sons of the Father in complete equality with the Son according to the essence of divinity. Rather, we are sons of the Father in complete equality according to the richness of God's love, who loves us with the same love with which He loves His only Son, even though none of us is the only Son, but we are children by grace.

The Infinite Divine Love and Human Unity

In this reflection, we come to appreciate the boundless righteousness of God, who loves all creatures out of nothing with the same profound love He holds for His Son. This divine love does not wane or diminish, even though there is a difference between the only-begotten Son and the believers. God's love transcends the limitations of human understanding, where love is often measured by quantity or quality. Instead, divine love is abundant and unfaltering. For this reason, the Lord Jesus Christ prayed, *"That the love with which You loved Me may be in them, and I in them"* (John. 17:26), and He also affirmed, *"You have loved them as You have loved Me"* (John.17:23). As the Apostle Paul wrote, *"But God demonstrates His own love toward us, in that while we were still sinners, Christ died for us"* (Rom. 5:8). This truth amazes the heavenly powers, as they witness those made from the dust of the earth being embraced by an eternal, undivided love, making the creature beloved in a manner akin to the Creator. This love is not about essence but about a profound, abiding affection shared within the Trinity.

Regarding the essence of the divine nature, the Trinity is equal. Each Person of the Trinity is equal in nature. However, the distinction among the Persons does not imply a hierarchy of greater or lesser, first or last. The distinction of the Persons is the source of incredible grace. As Jesus said, "*I and the Father are one*" (John 10:30), and as the Apostle Peter noted, "*The Spirit of glory and of God rests upon you*" (1 Peter. 4:14). Just as the Trinity preserves the distinction of the Persons through the unity of essence, it maintains the distinction between humans and the divine Persons through the purpose of grace and the unity of love. The goal of grace is growth, as Paul wrote, "*But grow in the grace and knowledge of our Lord and Saviour Jesus Christ*" (2 Peter. 3:18), and the purpose of love's unity is that we might become like Jesus, the "*Firstborn*," as Paul explained, "*For those God foreknew he also predestined to be conformed to the image of his Son*" (Rom. 8:29).

As we grow in grace, we are glorified according to the glory of Jesus Christ, becoming like Him as He became like us. He took on our human nature and, in turn, shared with us His divinity and son-ship, as revealed through His human nature with which we are united in the divine mysteries.

we are glorified in Him and become one Body with Him. As Paul wrote, "*Because there is one bread, we who are many are one body, for we all share the one bread*" (1 Cor. 10:17). Therefore, it is essential to ask why this unity occurs rather than how it happens. When we unite with His Body, we become one Body with Him. The unity among believers is a strength that reflects a heavenly, not an earthly, unity. While it may seem impossible for multiple entities to form a single body, by grace, the one Body has no distance separating it from its members. Distance applies to all visible phenomena, whereas unity is a matter of the heavenly and new creation. Each believer is a member, and the Body remains complete and whole even in the resurrection. As Paul declared, *"Now you are the body of Christ, and each one of you is a part of it"* (1 Cor. 12:27). Although we are many members, we are one Body, and our bodies are not reduced to a single member within the Lord's Body but remain whole. Our communion in Christ is through the Holy Spirit, who unites the members with the Lord, creating "*one Body*," which is the Body of Christ.

This unity is not a feature of physical bodies, nor is it contributed to by the members. Rather, it is a gift of the Holy Spirit, who transcends distances, sizes, and shapes. As Paul wrote, *"For in one Spirit we were all baptized into one body"* (1 Cor. 12:13). The Holy Spirit, as the Spirit of the Lord, gathers all despite physical distances. This union does not split into two: human and divine, but remains a single entity by the power of His union. Because He is undivided, He shares His life with believers, giving His Body and Blood fully to each communicant, as He distributed them in the Upper Room in Zion. As the Apostle John wrote, *"And the Word became flesh and dwelt among us"* (John.1:14), we partake in the divine mystery, becoming one with Him in a unity that defies earthly comprehension.

Understanding the Divine Mystery of Adoption

As we have previously discussed, we should focus on "*why?*" rather than "*how?*" because "*why?*" leads us into the depths of the divine plan of salvation. "*How?*" only brings us face-to-face with the profound mystery of God's love—a mystery that is the most sacred aspect of our faith, accessible only to those who have purified their minds from the constraints and characteristics of the original creation.

Why do we share in the son-ship of the eternal Son?

We were created from nothing, and our existence is fragile. Our participation in this divine communion is not self-sustaining but is dependent on the will and power of God. This is why we quickly lose what we receive. In Adam, humanity fell from a heavenly state, being made in the image and likeness of God. The Lord, in His grace, established four fundamental pillars of salvation:

Firstly, He made union with God the ultimate goal of the new creation.

Secondly, He granted us a share in the transformation that took place in His own human nature.

Thirdly, He secured grace through the gift and indwelling of the Holy Spirit. Thus, our salvation is no longer a product of our own efforts or willpower but is upheld by the strength of divine grace, according to God's goodness rather than our deeds.

Fourthly, He elevated us from the image and likeness of God in Adam to the complete and victorious image and likeness — an original state that Adam was intended to achieve through genuine transformation into the image of the Son, had he remained in holiness and communion. When Adam failed and fell, the Son came to restore Adam and his descendants to their original dignity.

These are the reasons for the gift of son-ship: by uniting with the incarnate Son, we partake in the glory of His humanity, which He achieved through His birth, baptism, crucifixion, resurrection, and ascension. These transformations in human nature were taken from the Virgin and were not created from nothing but were vivified by the Holy Spirit. He consecrated this nature in the Jordan with the power and grace of the Holy Spirit, anointing it for our benefit, so it might be preserved within Him. He overcame death on the cross, defeated corruption in the tomb, and vanquished the abyss with the radiance of His divine nature, rising to grant eternal life to all of humanity: body and soul. The separation of soul from body caused by death was abolished by the power of the union of His body and soul with His divinity. He ascended to heaven and sat at the right hand of the Father, revealing to us the ultimate purpose of existence in the heavenly dwellings, as He said, *"In My Father's house are many mansions"* (John 14:2).

This monumental transformation comes from the Lord and remains in Him; it is not subject to the will of the first Adam but is established by the will of the new Adam, our Lord Jesus Christ, our Saviour. This union was achieved *"without confusion, mixture, or change,"* preserving the distinction of the two natures while making them one in Him. Death could not separate the divine from the human nature, nor could weakness and corruption prevail over this union. Therefore, as we follow the example of the apostles, we seek to understand the reasons behind the divine plan, standing at the threshold of the sacred mysteries of faith. We ask the Lord to purify our minds from material distractions so that we may avoid the errors and sins of heretics.

Adoption and Participation in the Divine Nature

Sin does not shed light on grace, nor does it reveal the compassion and goodness of God. As the Evangelist writes, *"Sin is lawlessness"* (1 John.3:4), and lawlessness does not reveal the nature of God. Heretics fall into this diabolical trap, leading them away from the truth.

Arius denied the divinity of the Son because he adhered only to the law and rejected the grace of

God. Macedonius denied the divinity of the Holy Spirit, valuing the Spirit's gifts over the Spirit's person and over the love of God. Nestorius denied the union of divine and human natures in Christ, believing that human nature was too insignificant and frail for God to unite with and make one with Himself.

These heretics overlook the fact that the foundation of salvation – *"the pillar and ground of truth"* (1 Tim. 3:15) – is the one body of our Lord Jesus Christ, *"the firstborn among many brethren"* (Rom. 8:29). According to Christian belief, the Father's love for His incarnate, crucified, and ever-living Son is not merely a love for His divine nature but a single, inclusive love that embraces His humanity. As Paul writes, *"In this the love of God was made manifest among us, that God sent his only Son into the world, so that we might live through him"* (1 John 4:9).

The glory of the only Son does not divide into divine glory and human glory. Man, without God, is empty and dead, as it is written, *"If anyone does not have the Spirit of Christ, he does not belong to him"* (Rom. 8:9). The life of the incarnate Son is one unified, embodied life. The division and separation that heretics advocate only serve to isolate the Son – as God – from the Church, His body, rendering the Church headless, powerless, and lifeless. The Apostle Paul emphasizes this unity: *"The head of every man is Christ, the head of a wife is her husband, and the head of Christ is God"* (1 Cor. 11:3).

Heretical teachings begin with sin and end with what sin brings: transgression, death, and separation from God. These views wrongly carry over the consequences of separation into the concept of grace, imagining – based on human speculation rather than faith – that God abandons humanity in the pit of sin and death. The Apostle emphasizes the unity of sin and death: *"And you, who were dead in your trespasses and the un-circumcision of your flesh, God made alive together with him, having forgiven us all our trespasses*" (Col. 2:13). This confirms that forgiveness restores the grace of life that we lost through sin. Similarly, while death signifies separation from the source of life, grace brings humanity to life through the Holy Spirit in Jesus Christ forever: *"For as in Adam all die, so also in Christ shall all be made alive"* (1 Cor. 15:22).

When we discuss salvation starting from sin, we fall into three critical errors:

- We limit our understanding to the fallen state of humanity that we already know well. This error overlooks the transformative power of salvation that Paul describes: *"Therefore, if anyone is in Christ, he is a new creation. The old has passed away; behold, the new has come"* (2 Cor. 5:17).

- We judge human destiny based on the current state of death. This view contradicts Jesus' assurance: *"I am the resurrection and the life. Whoever believes in me, though he die, yet shall he live"* (John.11:25).

- We misapply the law's judgment, as stated by the Apostle: *"For the wages of sin is death"* (Rom. 6:23), wrongly placing new wine in old wineskins and new patches on old garments. Jesus warned against this approach, saying, *"No one puts new wine into old wineskins. If he does, the wine will burst the skins, and the wine is destroyed, and so are the skins"* (Mark 2:22).

The Apostle presents the plan of salvation as the cornerstone of the Gospel of life. The comparison between Jesus as the new Adam and the old Adam highlights the contrast between grace, life, and goodness, and the fall, death, and judgment. It starts with grace, affirming that where sin abounded, grace abounded even more: *"But where sin increased, grace abounded all the more"* (Rom. 5:20). This demonstrates that sin cannot be compared to grace.

Death does not reveal life; like sin, it represents a state of what we know well after the fall and does not showcase the power of eternal life found in our Lord Jesus Christ. Death introduced an overemphasis on bodily love and material things. With death came spiritual corruption: separation, hatred, and enmity. Our enmity with God became apparent because, due to our separation from Him, we wrongly believed that immortality could be achieved through our own efforts. Immortality is a gift, as Paul explains: *"The gift of God is eternal life in Christ Jesus our Lord"* (Rom. 6:23). We rejected the giver and sought to *"steal divinity,"* as the first Adam did by seeking equality with God and desiring forbidden knowledge (Gen. 3:5). But the true Son, who is equal to the Father in essence, came in the form of a servant to abolish the pride and enmity sown by the first Adam. As Paul writes, *"Have this mind among yourselves, which is yours in Christ Jesus, who, though he was in the form of God, did not count equality with God a thing to be grasped"* (Phil. 2:5-6).

Death presents three significant obstacles to our spiritual growth:

- It creates the illusion that we can achieve eternal life on our own, leading us to fear pain, illness, and loss. But Jesus assures us,

"Come to me, all who labour and are heavy laden, and I will give you rest" (Matt. 11:28).

- It encourages excessive love for the physical body, blinding us to the true existence that is in the image of God and in fellowship with Him who is the source of all life. As Jesus said, *"It is the Spirit who gives life; the flesh is no help at all"* (John 6:63).

- It misleads us into thinking that sin brings victory, happiness, and permanence, whereas it actually represents a violation of the divine nature and boundaries set by God. *"For everyone who makes a practice of sinning also practices lawlessness; sin is lawlessness"* (1 John.3:4).

Therefore, the discussion has addressed the *"hidden malady"* that compels individuals to prioritize their own lives over others. This *"hidden malady"* fosters greed, selfishness, envy, and other vices, all of which are false hopes of immortality that we endlessly seek. Instead, let us turn to Christ, who offers true life and grace.

The Advent of the Living God

Thus, the Living God, the Giver of Life, our Lord Jesus Christ, came to us, bringing peace with the Father. He dismantled every human misconception and proclaimed Himself as *"the Resurrection and the Life"* (John 11:25). By defeating death, He transformed its nature from a force of destruction to life into a means of overcoming sin. As He said, *"For the wages of sin is death, but the gift of God is eternal life in Christ Jesus our Lord"* (Rom.6:23). On the cross, He turned this hidden affliction into a power for repentance, making suffering and pain a path to salvation. He crucified greed through generosity, selfishness through bearing the cross, envy through love, and immorality through the sanctity of fellowship. He poured His life into us, leading the evangelist to exclaim, *"Whoever is born of God does not sin"* (1 John.3:9). In this way, He revealed the Lord's life within us — a life that originates from the Father in the Son through the power and action of the Holy Spirit.

We share in the Son's divine son-ship in the following ways, as much as human language and understanding can convey:

Firstly: Through the birth of the Lord from the Virgin Mary, human nature was elevated from nothingness to the realm of the Holy Spirit, the source of all creation's life. This is in accordance with the prophecy: *"The Holy Spirit will come upon you, and the power of the Most High will overshadow you; therefore the child to be born will be called holy — the Son of God"* (Luke.1:35).

Secondly: Through baptism, He anointed human nature and bestowed upon us the anointing of truth and holiness — the Spirit of truth, the Comforter, the Spirit of the Son, and the Spirit of holiness who *"raised Jesus from the dead"* (Rom.8:11). This sacrament of initiation transforms us, as Paul writes, *"We were therefore buried with him through baptism into death in order that, just as Christ was raised from the dead through the glory of the Father, we too may live a new life"* (Rom. 6:4). By this, He elevated the new human nature from mere intellectual consideration and willpower to the realm of holiness and life, granting it eternal stability.

Thirdly: On the cross, He abolished death and overcame it through His own death. He nailed death to the cross within us, turning it from a consequence of sin into a force working in us for repentance and life. As Paul states, "*He disarmed the powers and authorities, he made a public spectacle of them, triumphing over them by the cross*" (Col. 2:15).

Thus, death was transformed into a means of salvation, no longer separating the soul from the body, but rather separating the entire person from sin. Death became the death of Jesus, not the death of the first Adam, and transformed into a power of salvation.

Fourthly: Through His holy resurrection, He granted us immortality, overcame the corruption of the body, closed the abyss, and nullified judgment and the decree of death. As it is written, "*But Christ has indeed been raised from the dead, the first fruits of those who have fallen asleep*" (1 Cor.15:20). Therefore, these extraordinary gifts, moving from the old nature to the new creation, and witness our return to God through the Holy Spirit. From the counsel and thought of Adam to the wisdom and work of the Holy Spirit, and from life under judgment to an immortal life through the self-sacrifice of body and soul on the cross, so that the power of the Lord's resurrection and the presence of the Holy Spirit may be fully manifested.

Fifthly: What does the apostle mean by "*that Christ may dwell in your hearts through faith*" (Eph.3:17)? The Lord dwells in us because He first dwelt in the body He took from the Virgin, marking the beginning of His presence within us. "*Dwelling*" signifies an initiation, while "*indwelling*" implies permanence. We should avoid quarrelling over words, as the essence of both terms is captured in "*fellowship*," which clarifies their meanings. As John writes, *"And truly our fellowship is with the Father and with His Son Jesus Christ"* (1 John 1:3).

We share in the Lord according to His grace, not according to our desires or abilities. The Lord's grace was revealed in His acceptance of our human flesh eternally, establishing Him as the head of the new creation through the power of the Holy Spirit. As Paul says, *"For it is by grace you have been saved, through faith — and this is not from yourselves, it is the gift of God"* (Eph.2:8). When we share in the Lord by His grace, our own will and even the Lord's will alone do not become the cause of our salvation. Instead, it is the union of both wills, exemplified in the union of the two wills in the incarnate Son, that preserves and renews our freedom, guiding it continually towards eternal life.

Our Need for Christ's Indwelling

We do not worship in the manner of the nations; instead, we serve as the heavenly hosts serve. Our service is not motivated by a quest for rewards, as one might expect of slaves, but by a desire to live as children of God. The ultimate reward and prize is receiving what the Lord came to offer us, which is not earned through our own efforts. Our true inheritance is the Lord Himself. As the apostle Paul writes, *"Now if we are children, then we are heirs — heirs of God and co-heirs with Christ"* (Rom. 8:17). But what exactly will we inherit? Paul further explains, *"If we are children, then we are heirs — heirs of God and co-heirs with Christ"* (Rom. 8:17). When Peter speaks of an *"inheritance that is imperishable, undefiled, and unfading"* (1 Pet. 1:4), he is referring to God Himself (2 Peter. 1:4).

Christianity fundamentally differs from other faiths. According to the gospel, we do not receive or inherit anything other than God Himself. The Scriptures use terms like *"eternal life,"* *"the kingdom of heaven,"* and *"the kingdom of God"* to describe this singular divine gift. For instance, Jesus said, *"This is eternal life: that they know you, the only true God, and Jesus Christ, whom you have sent"* (John.17:3). Eternal life is found in the eternal God, and our fellowship with Him through Christ is what constitutes eternal life. Similarly, the kingdom of heaven is where God reigns, and it is where we will also reign as His children. Jesus affirmed, *"Blessed are the meek, for they will inherit the earth"* (Matt. 5:5).

So we must not to seek anything other than God Himself. Seeking gifts or blessings apart from God can lead to spiritual downfall. As it is written, *"What good will it be for someone to gain the whole world, yet forfeit their soul?"* (Matt.16:26). Possessing anything without God leads to ruin, but possessing everything with and through God means inheriting eternal life. *"But seek first his kingdom and his righteousness, and all these things will be given to you as well"* (Matt. 6:33).

We are not given mere *"things"* or *"attributes,"* nor do we share in God's attributes in a superficial way. Such notions are foreign to the gospel. The Lord Jesus did not come to give us attributes or tangible or intangible things. Instead, He declared, *"I have come that they may have life, and have it to the full"* (John 10:10).

Our primary calling is to live. As Peter writes, we are *"partakers of the divine nature"* (2 Peter.1:4). This concept transcends Greek philosophical distinctions between life and nature. When we say we are created in the image of God, the gospel speaks of the person or hypostasis. Sin turns us from persons (*hypostases*) into mere things. Desire drives us to seek what is impersonal (*non-hypostatic*), distancing us from the fellowship God intends.

Jesus came incarnate to embody human nature and elevate it from a state of death and corrupt imagination to a nature shaped by love. This is reflected in the scriptures, *"For we do not have a high priest who is unable to empathize with our weaknesses, but we have one who has been tempted in every way, just as we are—yet he did not sin"* (Heb. 4:15). Even when we say we are *"partakers of the divine nature,"* as Jesus declared, *"You are gods"* (John.10:34-35), this does not imply a change in human nature but a renewal of the divine image to reflect God's likeness. This renewal is not about acquiring attributes but about being transformed by love. Paul writes, *"But the fruit of the Spirit is love, joy, peace, forbearance, kindness, goodness, faithfulness, gentleness and self-control"* (Gal. 5:22-23), which elevates us to a life where the divine person governs and embraces nature freely.

The Lord became incarnate to restore the body's dignity, corrupted by sin, and to renew it through the grace of resurrection received in baptism and chrismation. As Paul states, *"We were therefore buried with him through baptism into death in order that, just as Christ was raised from the dead through the glory of the Father, we too may live a new life"* (Rom.6:4). When our hearts recognize that the body is alive forever in Christ and has received the grace of resurrection, this grace transforms it into beauty and freedom. It does not make the body a slave but embraces it in love as an offering to God, bearing the renewed image of God in Christ. This transformation is through the Holy Spirit and living according to the commandments of the gospel. As Paul exhorts, *"Therefore, I urge you, brothers and sisters, in view of God's mercy, to offer your bodies as a living sacrifice, holy and pleasing to God—this is your true and proper worship"* (Rom. 12:1).

When the soul drinks from the wellspring of divine love, it receives a sanctification that makes it heavenly and pure, reflecting the purity of the Bridegroom, our Lord Jesus Christ. As John writes, *"Dear friends, now we are children of God, and what we will be has not yet been made known. But we know that when Christ appears, we shall be like him, for we shall see him as he is"* (1 John.3:2).

When nations reject our Lord Jesus Christ as the Saviour and present intellectual arguments to prove that He is merely a created being and one of the prophets, they are essentially dividing their inheritance into two parts. The first part, which we share with them, is the humanity of the Lord, which aligns with our human nature according to the divine plan. The second part, which they oppose, is His divinity, equal to the Father in the unity of the divine essence. By rejecting this divine nature, they forfeit both aspects of the inheritance and fall under the judgment of rejecting salvation.

The first part, is of no value on its own. There is no true inheritance for humanity without God, no eternity without the eternal, living God, and no life without the source of life who overcomes death rather than being overcome by it. The Apostle Paul underscores this in 1 Corinthians 15:17, saying, *"And if Christ has not been raised, your faith is futile; you are still in your sins."* We inherit nothing from prophets or all humans, for created nature, which comes from nothing, does not possess itself. It is held by the Creator, depending on Him for existence, life, and movement (Acts. 17:28, *"For in Him we live and move and have our being"*).

Therefore, nations inherit nothing in Christ's kingdom without sharing in His life and accepting Him as Lord, Savior, and the new Head of salvation. John 1:12 confirms this: *"But to all who did receive*

Him, who believed in His name, He gave the right to become children of God."

Believing in the Lord Jesus merely as a human does not constitute true faith. As humans, we understand what humanity is and do not need to acknowledge Him merely as human like us. Even recognizing Him as a prophet brings no benefit, as it replaces the grace of the Gospel with the law. Jesus Himself addressed this in John 14:6: *"I am the way, and the truth, and the life. No one comes to the Father except through Me."* Therefore, we must confidently proclaim, with the same faith preached by the apostles: *"If righteousness could be achieved through the law, then Christ died for no reason"* (Gal. 2:21).

Christ Jesus: The Source of Our New Life

When the Son of God, our Lord Jesus Christ, renewed humanity, He transformed it from death into life. He became the *"first,"* the *"firstborn,"* and the *"beginning"*—all terms that underscore His supreme position. He is the *"first"* because He is the new Adam; He is the *"firstborn"* because He has *"many brothers"* (Rom. 8:29), as Paul the Apostle affirms. He is the *"beginning"* because He alone can provide a fresh start and new life to those who have been dominated by death. This renewal is essential, as Jesus Himself declared in Revelation 21:5: *"Behold, I am making all things new."*

The Apostle Paul contrasts the first Adam with the last Adam, stating, *"The first man was from the earth, a living being"* (1 Cor. 15:45), while *"the last Adam"* is a *"life-giving spirit"* (1 Cor. 15:45). Paul further explains, *"Just as we have borne the image of the earthly man, so shall we bear the image of the heavenly man"* (1 Cor. 15:49). This new image is not based on earthly standards or *"human sense,"* which cannot fully grasp the divine gift of God's image, but is according to Christ. As it is written in Colossians 3:10, *"And have put on the new self, which is being renewed in knowledge after the image of its creator."* We experience this transformation through the sacraments and witness it clearly in the prayers and hymns of the Church.

Paul's reference to *"a living being"* denotes the earthly life we share with other creatures. If we confine ourselves to this earthly existence, we become merely earthly beings. This is evident in a life driven by the pleasures of the flesh and sins that cut us off from true life, turning us into beings who are content with envy, anger, murder, adultery, lying, and other sins that kill the soul, or human life. As it is stated in Galatians 5:19-21, *"The works of the flesh are evident: sexual immorality, impurity, sensuality, idolatry, sorcery, enmity, strife, jealousy, fits of anger, rivalries, dissensions, divisions, envy, drunkenness, orgies, and things like these."*

The death of the soul through sin becomes apparent when we observe the decline of our inner spiritual faculties, such as perception and reasoning—understanding, imagination, and intelligence. When these faculties are ruled by desires, they become conflicted, weakening the will, separating the mind from the body, and sometimes turning the body into a mere instrument through which the soul seeks fulfilment, despite the body being the soul's visible and inseparable aspect. Romans 7:23 describes this conflict: *"But I see in my members another law waging war against the law of my mind and making me captive to the law of sin that dwells in my members."*

One of the most critical aspects of spiritual death is the ignorance of the Creator and the inability to recognize that He fills everything: heaven and earth. This ignorance is addressed through ascetic practices like constant prayer, immersion in the Scriptures, and service to others. Jesus said in John 17:3, *"And this is eternal life, that they know You, the only true God, and Jesus Christ whom You have sent."* Such practices counteract ignorance and allow the light of divine knowledge, given by the Spirit of wisdom, the Spirit of Jesus Christ, the Holy Spirit, to shine through. As 2 Corinthians 4:6 declares, *"For God, who said, 'Let light shine out of darkness,' has shone in our hearts to give the light of the knowledge of the glory of God in the face of Jesus Christ."* Thus, according to the apostolic teaching, our new birth begins with enlightenment and the illumination of divine knowledge, enabling us to overcome ignorance and embrace our new life in Christ.

The New Life We Receive from Our Lord Jesus Christ

Due to death's dominion over humanity, we required someone who embodies *"life"* itself and possesses the creative power to grant life anew and abolish death — the hidden affliction that is the root and source of sin. The Son of the living God, the second Person of the Trinity, the Word, and the only Son, who is life itself, came to us. He is *"the Son"* by His divine nature, *"equal to the Father in essence,"* and one with the Holy Trinity (John.1:4, 14; John.10:30).

When we refer to these divine titles and attributes, we emphasize the power of the Redeemer and Saviour, the Lord of Heaven and Earth, who appeared in our human form and united with us through the human nature He took from the Holy and Pure, Mary (Luke.1:35).

- He is the Son, while by nature, we are enslaved and bound by sin (Rom. 6:16-17).

- He is the Word, while by nature, we are ignorant of God and live in darkness (John.1:5, 9).

- He is equal to the Father, while we are not equal to the Father, nor are we equal to anything, as we were created from nothing and lack an inherent existence capable of enduring by itself (Acts 17:28-29).

- He is the Son of God, and we— as the Apostle Paul said— were "*by nature children of wrath*" (Eph. 2:3). Thus, the Son embraced all these divine attributes in His name "*Jesus*," which means "*Yahweh saves*" (Matt. 1:21), because He came to rescue us from our deep-seated sins and harsh bondage (Luke.4:18).

When we say "*Lord Jesus Christ,*" we encapsulate everything we believe in these two words. We receive new life directly from the Lord Jesus, as revealed through the heavenly mysteries. In the sacrament of Baptism, as instituted by the holy Apostles, we transition from the servitude of the first Adam— from human nature— to a nature destined to be a new creation. According to the Apostle's pious words, we are "*formed into Christ*" (Gal. 4:19), meaning we become an image of Christ (2 Cor. 3:18).

After Adam failed to be the "*image of God*" (Gen. 1:26-27), the Lord came and recreated us in His own image— the image of the divine union with humanity. He conquered death through His own death and renewed us in His Person, making our human nature His own divine nature. This nature does not live independently of the divinity or separate from it, as the heretics claimed, but is united with it according to the apostolic tradition we received from the Lord and the Apostles. This tradition affirms our salvation in Christ Jesus and the union with Him, and what our once bare humanity has gained— clothed with the divine glory, power, and life, and sharing in communion with the Father and the Holy Spirit (1 Cor. 15:22-23; Col. 2:9).

Thus, the only Son of God began with adoption and completed the plan of salvation by ascending to Heaven (Acts.1:9-11).We cannot fully define the new life because— as the Apostle said— it "*is not of this creation*" (Heb.11:9), not "*of flesh and blood and human will*" (John.1:13), but from above. It is challenging to describe it in detail as we discuss earthly matters. However, the Lord Jesus, the Teacher of Truth, being "*the Truth incarnate*" (John 14:6), revealed this life to us through His incarnate divine existence.

From divinity, humanity received everything. Though born of the Virgin Mary as true God and true man, one with the Father in divinity and one with us in humanity, equal to the Father in divinity, and equal to us in the plan of salvation, He established the beginning of His human life not according to the old creation— physical birth through the flesh and marriage—but according to the new creation— birth through the Holy Spirit (Luke.1:35). Thus, He was born of the Holy Spirit and the Virgin Mary, the Mother of God, as a complete human in every respect— except for sin— with a body, rational soul, will, speech, and complete bodily functions, being the new Adam (Rom. 5:14; Heb. 4:15).

When He united divinity and humanity in His one Person, that is, the only-begotten Son of God who became incarnate according to the divine plan, He introduced for the first time in history the union of divinity with humanity and made this union the beginning of the new human race. Therefore, the inheritance of the new creation is our union with God according to the incarnation, meaning that we remain human as the Son's humanity remained, and that we continue to be created from the first Adam as the Son's humanity was created, but with the creative power of the Trinity, which is revealed in baptism, where we are born into a new spiritual life for both soul and body (Titus 3:5; John 3:5).

Therein, we receive the pledge of the resurrection of the Lord Jesus Christ, "*awaiting adoption, the redemption of our bodies*" (Rom. 8:23). Thus, the Apostle says, "*born again, not of corruptible seed (of man), but of incorruptible, by the word of God which lives and abides forever (the creative power); for all flesh is as grass, and all the glory of man as the flower of the grass; the grass withers, and its flower falls away. But the word of the Lord endures forever. And this is the word which by the gospel was preached to you*" (1 Peter. 1:23-25).

As the Lord Jesus explained to the teacher of Israel, our second birth comes not through a return to biological birth, but through a spiritual rebirth from God. This rebirth is from the divine power that imparts life—our living Lord and the Holy Spirit. Through the Holy Spirit, we are baptized and receive the divine seal on our bodies. This seal, conferred through the chrism, is marked on the members of the body that correspond to the human spirit. Every part of our physical body has its origin in the spirit or soul. It represents the spirit or soul, expresses its movement and vitality, and reveals it in us. The body is the visible manifestation (or icon) of the human spirit. The absence or removal of some body parts does not mean the destruction of the spirit's essence; rather, the spirit's essence remains, awaiting the completion of creation on the day of our final resurrection, which we eagerly anticipate with joy and patience. Hence, the Apostle proclaims this future grace that has been established in us and will be revealed on the day of the Lord's judgment: *"Set your hope fully on the grace that will be brought to you at the revelation of Jesus Christ"* (1 Peter 1:13).

In reflecting on the profound understanding of the human body as a divine gift, it is noted that such a perspective recognizes the body as a manifestation of the incarnate God. This appreciation endures through times of trial and continues even after death, with the anticipation of a future transformation. Ultimately, this transformation promises that our humble bodies will be transformed to reflect the glorious nature of the divine.

The New Birth through the Sacrament of Baptism

It is crucial not to misinterpret the Apostle Peter's words. The living and enduring word of God is the power of the Trinity, the rational principle or Logos, by which the Trinity created the heavens and the earth. When we grasp this power as revealed in the scriptures, we hear the prophets say: *"God said, 'Let there be...'"* (Gen. 1:3). God does not speak in a specific language; the act of creation is conveyed to us according to our understanding. On the day of Pentecost, when the apostles spoke in various languages, the Holy Spirit revealed that God does not have a particular language. Instead, the language of the Holy Spirit is truth, which is the Son. The Son's incarnation granted us the freedom to use all languages, affirming that His incarnation would be fulfilled on Pentecost.

The apostles preached even in the languages of Arabs, Greeks, and others. Truth came without a specific language or words to those capable of grasping it beyond words, through the vision of the Holy Spirit which allows us to understand what the Spirit sees in God and what transcends verbal expression.

However, because we are still in the body, our capacity for speech and understanding relies on words. Spiritual perception must rise and enter into the realm of the Holy Spirit, experiencing the vision of what is and what will be according to the Spirit's revelation. When we chant the cherubic hymn in church—"Holy, Holy, Holy, Lord of Sabaoth"—each church sings it in its own language. What unites these languages is not the words themselves but the holiness of the Holy Trinity that transcends words and letters. We understand this holiness through the sanctification of the body and soul by the Holy Spirit, elevating us to join in heavenly praise.

For this reason—our freedom in worship according to the Holy Spirit—we do not repeat the exact words of the Lord in the Eucharist. He gave thanks, but the apostles did not pass on those words of thanks to us. The sacrament's power lies not in the words spoken by the Lord but in the gift given; the gift of the body and blood surpasses all words. We are not magicians reciting special words with inherent power, but we worship and serve the Trinity according to the grace revealed to us. The sacramental words: *"Thank you, bless, and sanctify"* are not confined to specific words but are arranged according to the order of the Spirit of Life, transcending mere verbal limits. Thanksgiving and blessing belong to the high priest, while sanctification belongs to the Holy Spirit who serves the mysteries of the Son, taking from what belongs to Him and giving to the Church (John 14:16, 15). All of this is one service to the Holy Trinity

Understanding Truth and the New Covenant

Truth is not simply declared through words; it is signalled by symbols and indicators, because truth is embodied in the Incarnate Son. The Incarnation was not about words but about the Word becoming flesh, transforming into signs and symbols of truth — essentially, His divine person. As the Apostle John writes, *"And the Word became flesh and dwelt among us"* (John 1:14). This incarnate Word embodies the ultimate revelation of truth.

The contrast between the Old and New Testaments is profound. The Ten Commandments were not just words etched on stone tablets; they became the cornerstone of a new law — the law of life. This new law is written through perfect union with the Son's life and by the grace of the Holy Spirit, who serves the Son's mysteries, reveals the Trinity, and guides creation towards the Father. As Paul explains, *"For the law of the Spirit of life in Christ Jesus has made me free from the law of sin and death"* (Rom. 8:2). Unlike the Old Testament, where murder was viewed as *"slaughter"* (Exod. 20:13), the Holy Spirit now heals the human heart from the anger that leads to murder, which is often fuelled by pride (Gal. 5:20).

The Holy Spirit nurtures both humility in Christ and the love of the Father, stabilizing the soul and body and aligning all human faculties with the eternal life to come, thereby eradicating pride and anger.

Thus, the conflict is no longer between humans and the stone tablets engraved with the law. Instead, it is a matter of the heart striving to grasp the truth through sanctification and love. This is not an intellectual or subjective endeavour originating from man but a participation in the Lord's life, His life-giving death, and His resurrection. This participation is rooted in the incarnate Son, sourced from the Father, and sustained by the Holy Spirit in its power and sanctity. As Paul writes, *"For as many as are led by the Spirit of God, these are sons of God"* (Rom. 8:14).

When the Apostle Paul refers to Christ as the *"last Adam"* and the *"Lord from heaven"* (1 Cor. 15:47), he establishes the foundation of the New Covenant. He confirms that the Lord is Adam, or the *"second man"* (1 Cor.15:45), and that He is both *"the Lord"* and *"from heaven."* This unbroken triad affirms the human foundation — namely, the Son's Incarnation — and the divine structure, which is the Lord's deity, and the heavenly structure created by the Holy Spirit (1 Cor. 15:47; Colo. 2:9). According to the Son's dispensation revealed in the Scriptures, the Lord came to us bearing the gift of eternal life, His own hypostatic life, which cannot be overcome by death but which triumphed over death on the cross (1 Cor. 15:54). As Jesus said, *"I am the resurrection and the life. He who believes in Me, though he may die, he shall live"* (John 11:25).

How did the Lord build this house? It was not constructed from this creation, which cannot provide eternal life. Anything that emerges from nothing and receives its existence from God can only possess eternal permanence through God's will. If it loses its life, it cannot regain it. We consume food to sustain our temporary earthly life, but this does not grant us eternal life. As the Apostle said, *"The stomach for foods and foods for the stomach, but God will destroy both it and them"* (1 Cor. 6:13). Everything is destined to perish according to its use. Therefore, the body, the visible form of the spirit, perishes, but the spirit does not perish due to our abilities, will, or even virtuous actions. It receives the gift of eternal life, which preserves it and restores the visible form of the spirit to a glorious resurrection according to the teaching of the Lord Jesus Christ. As Paul asserts, *"For our citizenship is in heaven, from which we also eagerly wait for the Saviour, the Lord Jesus Christ, who will transform our lowly body that it may be conformed to His glorious body"* (Phil. 3:20-21).

Thus, the foundation of the house is not earthly and perishable but remains forever by the power of the Lord, who has put everything under His feet (1 Cor. 15:27; Eph. 1:22; Heb. 2:8). He has absolute authority over all that is in heaven and on earth, uniting everything under one head, His divine headship and eternal sovereignty, for He is the eternal King. As Paul writes, *"He must reign till He has put all enemies under His feet"* (1 Cor. 15:25).

The heavenly foundation mirrors the structure itself; for the foundation is the Lord, the cornerstone is the Lord, and the rock is the Lord. Jesus said, *"On this rock I will build My church, and the gates of Hades shall not prevail against it"* (Matt. 16:18). The teachings of the Gnostics and Unitarians reveal that they are without foundation, house, or revelation. They only possess the law, which provides them with temporary earthly benefits in the life to come because they do not know the heavenly things.

When the Apostle mentioned being *"built upon the foundation of the apostles and prophets,"* he referred to the teaching and prophetic word as the *"shining lamp"* (2 Peter.1:19). However, the Lord is the *"Spirit of prophecy"* (Rev. 19:10), and the testimony of Jesus Christ our Lord is the culmination of prophecy. Therefore, the prophetic word was disconnected from Gnostic teachings because they do not know Isaiah, Jeremiah, or the other prophets, but only know Moses, the lawgiver. Moses received the stone tablets from God as the beginning of a teaching that should lead to completeness, which is the fullness that dwells physically in Christ (Col. 2:9), the Lord who *"fills all in all"* (Eph. 1:23).

When they reverted to the law, they indirectly rejected the mediation of the Creator Himself, the Word, the only Son of the Father. Their rejection stems from ignorance; the law does not lead to God but to spiritual weakness. It confines man within his understanding of the law concerning good and evil, establishing rituals that become iron bonds. It restricts the mind to seeking what is allowed and prohibited, aiming to fulfil what is possible. When individuals stumble and fall, they seek rituals of physical purification from this creation, which only cleanse the body while leaving the heart un-purified. Washings do not reach the heart, leaving the body clean but the mind and heart still tainted. As Jesus said, *"Woe to you, scribes and Pharisees, hypocrites! For you cleanse the outside of the cup and dish, but inside they are full of extortion and self-indulgence"* (Matt. 23:25).

The Nature of Salvation and the Role of Love

We believe that the one in whom *"all the fullness of the Deity lives in bodily form"* (Col. 2:9) came to us in perfect fellowship, which is grounded not in human goodness or wickedness but in the goodness and love of the Trinity. When we say that the Son took on human form and became sinless in the flesh, we affirm not only the sanctity of the Lord Jesus but also that sin is neither the cause nor the source of salvation. As it is written, *"For our sake he made him to be sin who knew no sin, so that in him we might become the righteousness of God"* (2 Cor. 5:21). Rather, it is God's goodness. He did not come merely to abolish the judgments of the law, as the Apostle said: *"He cancelled the written code, with its regulations, that was against us and that stood opposed to us"* (Col. 2:14). Instead, He came to demonstrate through His death and resurrection that salvation is a gift from God, received through faith, not by the works of the law. This way, no one can boast, as the Apostle explained (Eph. 2:9): *"Not by works, so that no one can boast."*

The Lord came to show that the true fulfilment of the law is found in love. *"Love does not negate what came before but rather fulfils and builds upon it"* (Matt. 5:17): *"Do not think that I have come to abolish the Law or the Prophets; I have not come to abolish them but to fulfil them."* This new foundation from God is rooted in the truth that God is love (1 John.4:8), and He is the ultimate source of all that is good. While the law reveals human transgression, love surpasses the law by offering renewal to those under its dominion, including death. The Lord died for sinners and the ungodly, as the Apostle Paul affirms: *"But God shows his love for us in that while we were still sinners, Christ died for us"* (Rom.5:8). When the prophet says: *"I am counted among the wicked"* (Is. 53:12), he subtly alludes to the Gnostics' errors and their ridicule of the cross's wisdom, dismissing the crucified and the cross as insignificant. As the Apostle noted, it is *"a scandal and foolishness"* (1 Corinthians 1:23). When he declared that *"the foolishness of God is wiser than human wisdom"* (1 Cor. 1:25), he underscored the world's inability to grasp the cross's wisdom, which involves selfless giving and sacrifice for those who do not deserve it.

The new birth happens in baptism through the power and work of the Holy Spirit, which unites us with the Son so that we may partake in His son-ship. As Scripture highlights: *"Jesus answered, 'Very truly I tell you, no one can see the kingdom of God unless they are born again*'" (John.3:3). When Scripture speaks of the new birth, it highlights two key points:

1. We do not give birth to ourselves. Just as children cannot birth themselves, it is the mother's power—symbolized here by the Holy Spirit—that births us in Christ. As it is written: "*For it is by grace you have been saved, through faith—and this is not from yourselves, it is the gift of God*" (Eph. 2:8).

2. Man cannot recreate or renew himself. We are born for the renewal prepared by the Lord Jesus, beginning with His incarnation (His union with us) and continuing through His baptism in the Jordan, where He received the Holy Spirit for our sake (Matt 3:16). This renewal reaches its peak in the defeat of death, the promise of immortality, the inheritance of eternal life, and the resurrection of the body (1 Cor.15:22). Thus, we must recognize that the new creation prepared by the Lord through His incarnation, baptism, crucifixion, resurrection, and ascension is the same process He is working in us. As we go through these stages in the "*inner man,*" we exist in the Lord Jesus through the mysteries of union, but we grow towards Him. We receive baptism as children, but we need the filling and anointing of the Holy Spirit, which we receive in the sacrament of chrismation (Acts 8:17). This anointing is further kindled through prayer, ascetic practices, and guarding the heart ,So we should always seek the "*fiery spirit,*".

Our life as Christians involves a daily effort to be crucified with the Lord. We pray with Him to rise with Him and in Him, being crucified so that we do not live a merely physical life, as the Apostle said: "*I have been crucified with Christ*" (Gal.2:20). This means the physical life has died, and according to the flesh, we are dead — evident in aging and decline. But dying with the Lord is a death we pursue willingly and lovingly, which is the "*bond of perfection*" (Col.3:14). Through love, we mortify the will. The greater prevails over the lesser: Christ, who is greater, over the present age, which passes away.

Christ lives in us in this way, and to the extent we can express it: He is the foundation of our new life, which may be unseen because it is hidden from the five senses (2 Cor. 4:18), preserving our freedom. He does not force Himself into our lives but gently leads us in His love toward the goal of salvation — union with the divine nature. When we say "*may be unseen*," it is because we walk by faith, not by sight (2 Cor. 5:7). Sometimes the Son of God may manifest visibly in us, but such manifestations are rare, even among saints. Seeking such signs is not harmful as long as it does not become our goal, which could limit our love (Matt. 12:39).

The Lord nourishes the inner man through the word, the teachings we hear from believers, and the love we practice, helping us grow spiritually from God toward God. This is the role of true knowledge, free from false teachings. We do not grow to earn God's favour or make Him love us more; we grow because He loved us first (1 John.4:19), even when we did not love Him, and reconciled us as enemies (Rom.5:10). We do not attain the kingdom of heaven through good works, as this would negate God's love for humanity, which He redeemed despite its fullness.

Christ heals our sins with His divine patience and with the patience of "*One who suffered being tempted, that He might be able to help those who are tempted*" (Heb.2:18). He endures all the weaknesses, falls, and sins of those who adhere to Him. Thus, the Apostle says that He "*is not ashamed to call us brothers*" (Heb. 2:11), affirming His special love even for the lost and wayward, as He seeks to bring us back to the fold (Luke.15:4-7).

In conclusion, the focus is on inviting Christ to dwell within everyone. This shared aspiration emphasizes the collective hope that Christ's presence will be a guiding and transformative force in all our lives. In our gatherings, the Lord commands the blessing, as the Psalm says: "*For there the Lord commanded the blessing, life forevermore*" (Ps. 133:3), and there He is present as teacher and healer according to the divine revelation: "*Where two or three are gathered in My name, there I am in the midst of them*" (Matt. 18:20). The Lord's presence among us is the wellspring of life that flows with the Holy Spirit, cleansing us from all impurity so we may share in the saints' fellowship.

And the communal prayer holds a special place in the heart of the divine Trinity, embodying the fellowship of eternal love. It is crucial to embrace and support the weak, as neglecting them can lead to serious consequences, while a lack of forgiveness is deeply disapproved. By strengthening the vulnerable with kindness and love, hidden pride is healed, and unity with the divine is fostered. Goodness and love are essential in nurturing this connection and fostering a supportive community.

It is essential to continually seek the Lord's mercy, both within and beyond the Prayers, to avoid the delusion of self-righteousness. Holding steadfast to the confession of true faith, as exemplified by the faithful who preceded us, remains the clear path to spiritual fulfilment and the fruits of the kingdom. Additionally, seeking the wisdom of the Gospel will guide our lives towards the harbour of salvation, in accordance with divine promises.

Jesus Christ is the same yesterday, today, and forever, unchanging. His love does not grow because of our love; rather, our love grows because of His love (Heb. 13:8).

The Lord is near to us, closer than our own hearts (Ps.34:18)

LOGOS ECHOES
WHEREVER LOGOS INSPIRE

Welcome To The Realm Of Logos

Where the profound realms of theology and spirituality intertwine, your journey of faith begins. Embark on a transformative quest for knowledge and spiritual growth as we offer a rich tapestry of E-books designed to nourish your soul and ignite your mind.

At the heart of Logos Echoes beats a passion for sharing the life-changing power of God's Word. We illuminate the timeless truths of Christianity with a fresh perspective, providing a captivating blend of deep theological insights and practical wisdom. By understanding the heart of God and the mind of Christ, we empower believers to live out their faith with confidence and purpose.

Our ministry is to ignite a flame within your heart, deepening your connection with Christ and equipping you to share His love with the world. Discover thought-provoking insights, practical guidance, and timeless truths that will transform your life, Through the life-changing message of Jesus Christ.

Together, we will unlock the boundless potential of your faith and experience the profound peace and fulfilment found in a deep relationship with Christ.

Waiting To Hear From You

If you find it worth it, please don't hesitate to contact us. Your feedback is like gold to us! These insights help us improve, grow, and create better Christian content for everyone. Share your thoughts and ideas with us. You are always welcome. And remember, our goal is:

TOGETHER WITH LOGOS,
WE MAKE THE WORLD BETTER

Email us: logosechoes@gmail.com

About the Author

Sameh Saied is A Researcher and Self-Published Author in the Field of Christian Studies, Particularly Focusing on the History of Early Christianity ,also the Founder of Logos Echoes Publications. His Aim is to Publish Works that address Theological, Biblical, and Spiritual Topics of interest to readers, to foster a deeper understanding of the Christian Faith, which is reflected in individual lives and society as a whole, by presenting diverse perspectives on the Bible and Christian Doctrines. Until now published four books:

- God Among Us: The Rational Case for the Incarnation.

- The Heart of Jesus: Unveiling His Eternal Love for Humanity.

- Restoring the Divine Participation: The Holy Spirit's Role and the Path to True Repentance.

- Recreating Humanity: Illuminating Our Divine Identity in Christ.